I0417210

Behavioral Momentum

A Scientific Metaphor

$$\Delta B = -x\,/\,m$$

In physics, Newton's second law:

$$\Delta v = f / m$$

Δv = change in velocity
f = imposed force

Any change of velocity is directly proportional to the imposed force and inversely proportional to the mass of the body

Translated into behavior:

$$\Delta B = -x / m$$

ΔB = change in behavioral response rate
x = value of the disruptor

a minus sign here because response rate decreases during disruption

m = Behavioral mass

Under constant conditions, behavioral response rates continue unchanged unless acted upon by an external disruptor. The magnitude of the decrease depends directly on the magnitude of the disruptor and inversely on the inferred behavioral mass imparted by the rate of reinforcement.

A Scientific Metaphor

John A. Nevin

MMXV

Copyright © 2015 John A. Nevin
Professor Emeritus
University of New Hampshire
Home: 20 Harborview Lane
Vineyard Haven, MA 02568
e-mail: tony.nevin@unh.edu
Printed in the USA · All Rights Reserved
ISBN-13 9781512297690 · ISBN-10 1512297690

Table of Contents

Introduction 1

Chapter 1
Review of Basic Concepts 13

Chapter 2
Research Methods and Measures .34

Chapter 3
Choice, Response Rate, and Resistance to Change 52

Chapter 4
The Momentum Metaphor. 76

Chapter 5
Operant and Pavlovian Determiners
of Resistance to Change. 94

Chapter 6
Challenges to Behavioral Momentum Theory. 121

Chapter 7
Extinction and Recovery. 139

Chapter 8
Resistance to Change of Discriminating,
Attending, and Remembering. .166

Chapter 9
Extensions to Clinical and Applied Settings 186

Postscript. 200

End Notes 205

Dedication

This book could not have been written without the many students, colleagues, and friends who joined me in gathering the data and developing the ideas described here. Their findings and insights were essential to the development of Behavioral Momentum Theory, and I have tried to acknowledge all of them in the following text. The entire process of engaging in research and theoretical conjecture with these enthusiastic collaborators has been great fun, and I thank them all.

Introduction

I have spent most of my professional life studying behavioral momentum – roughly speaking, the tendency of any activity, once in progress, to continue until interrupted or blocked in some way, much like a ball rolling down a slope. If the ball is heavy, it will roll unchecked over twigs lying in its path, but if the ball is light, it may be stopped or diverted from its course by those same twigs.

The persistence of the ball's motion is determined by current physical variables: its mass and velocity. The persistence of an organism's activities, however, can depend on certain events experienced in the distant past, known to the science of behavior as a "history of reinforcement." My research on the effects of history on behavioral persistence is itself the result of my history of reinforcement as a student, teacher, and researcher in behavioral science. Here are some of the critical events that affected the evolution of that research.

Personal history

I graduated from Yale University in 1954 with a degree in mechanical and marine engineering, then served in the US Coast Guard. While in the service, I had a lot of time to read, and by chance encountered the mid-19th-century work of G. T. Fechner, who had derived a simple equation relating the magnitude of a private sensory experience to the physical intensity of a stimulus from an empirical principle known as Weber's Law. I was excited by the idea that private experience could be measured by inference from a quantitative principle, and I could understand the math; so when I left the Coast Guard in 1959, I went to Columbia to study psychophysics – the relation between psychological experience and physical events.

It turned out to be a good move. Not having studied psychology previously, I had no preconceptions of the field, and felt right at home in graduate courses on mathematical and statistical models of psychophysics with Professor McGill (John Gibbon, whose later work inspired a component of behavioral momentum theory, was a fellow graduate student), and on sensory psychology with Professor Graham, with whom I did a project on color perception. But at the end of my first year, in 1960, I needed a paying job, and the only open position for a research assistant was in a project on the effects of drugs on animal discrimination and behavior. The project manager, Bob Berryman, hired me to build apparatus and conduct experiments and soon proposed that we do an experiment together. Bob had designed a piece of equipment to implement a so-called interlocking schedule of reinforcement, which bridged the conceptual gap between a fixed-interval schedule whereby a rat could get food for the first lever press after a given period of time, and a fixed-ratio schedule whereby food was obtained after a given number of responses (see Chapter 1). Bob's gimmick arranged a linear tradeoff of time and responses so that working faster made food available sooner, and the terms of the tradeoff – how many responses equaled how many seconds – had clear, orderly, continuous effects on the rats' rate of lever pressing.

When the data were all in hand, Bob suggested that we write them up for publication, and we sat before a clunky mechanical typewriter, discussing each sentence – sometimes each word – as the text unfolded. I loved the whole process, and I was being paid to do work that I loved, so I switched to the experimental analysis of behavior as my major field. I went on to work with Bill Cumming and Bob Berryman on a series of studies on delayed matching to sample in pigeons (more on this in Chapter 8), did a doctoral dissertation on secondary reinforcement (still a vexing topic) under the direction of Nat Schoenfeld, and learned to appreciate the joys of teaching from Fred Keller while he was developing his personalized system of instruction.

After completing the Ph.D. at Columbia in 1963, I taught at Swarthmore College for five years, with a year out as a research associate at Harvard with B. F. Skinner and Richard Herrnstein. I went back to Columbia in 1968 as a faculty member, mostly because I wanted to have graduate students; and for a mix of personal and professional reasons, I abandoned Columbia and moved to the University of New Hampshire in 1972. Most of my thinking about behavioral momentum developed as a result of teaching and collaborative research with undergraduates and graduate students at UNH, and I enjoyed every bit of it.

In 1995, UNH offered a favorable retirement deal; I accepted and moved with my wife to Martha's Vineyard, where we have a sailboat and participate in various community projects. Almost 20 years later, though, I'm still

3

doing the same sort of academic and scientific stuff that I did and loved since 1960: Applying for research funds, collaborating on research in other laboratories, staying up late analyzing data that colleagues send to me by e-mail attachment, looking for orderly relations that generalize broadly, and writing articles for academic journals, even though my retirement checks would keep coming if I just went sailing. That sounds suspiciously like a bad case of behavioral momentum – and it is possible that those retirement checks actually contribute to my academic persistence (see Chapter 5).

Acknowledgements

The research described in this book would not have come to fruition without the involvement, and friendship, of a number of colleagues. Here, I will name those who have most influenced the work on behavioral momentum. Charlotte Mandell, a graduate student at Columbia, moved with me to UNH as a Research Associate, helped to set up a new lab (within 24 hours of a U-Haul move of the equipment and pigeons!) and for ten years was closely involved in every aspect of my work. Bud Mace saw that the momentum metaphor was relevant to clinical interventions designed to ameliorate problem behavior, and got me involved – as a commentator, not a practitioner – in applied work. Randy Grace came to UNH as a graduate student, joined my lab after a seminar on learning and behavior theory, taught me how to do sophisticated quantitative data analyses, and contributed a novel perspective on behavioral momentum while managing the lab and making sure that the pigeons and apparatus were never idle. Anthony McLean brought another perspective when he visited UNH from the University of Canterbury in Christchurch, New Zealand; later, Randy joined the faculty at Canterbury and strengthened the New Hampshire-New Zealand connection, which had already been established for me by exchanging manuscripts and visits with Michael Davison and his students at the University of Auckland. Finally, after my retirement and Randy's departure for New Zealand, Amy Odum and Tim Shahan offered the use of their UNH lab for collaborative research, and our joint endeavors have continued since their move to Utah State University. In addition, at least two dozen students and colleagues have contributed in one way or another to the development and application of the metaphor of behavioral momentum, and I thank them all.

I also thank the National Science Foundation and the National Institutes of Health for many years of research support. If the work described here contributes to a fuller understanding of human behavior with data-based applications that contribute to better ways of living, their investment will be amply justified.

I acknowledge with pleasure the people who have helped me to assemble this book for publication. Janet Holladay, at The Tisbury Printer in Vineyard Haven, formatted three complete drafts to achieve the final product, and was always patient when I wanted changes, however minor. Paul Karasik, a *New Yorker* cartoonist who lives on Martha's Vineyard, designed the cover to give a graphic perspective on the momentum process and resistance to change. Many thanks, Janet and Paul.

And many thanks to my wife Nora, who tolerated my momentum-based neglect of her calls to dinner while I was typing away upstairs. Paul Karasik's cartoon (below) delightfully captures the reinforcing power of digital devices, including the persistence of my work on a laptop. Nora approves its appearance here.

Overview of this book

Let me begin by explaining what this book is not. First, it is not a textbook, although it could be used to accompany a more general text in advanced undergraduate or graduate courses. Second, it is not a literature review or an authoritative scholarly compendium of the relevant research literature; it concentrates on the development of my own work, from my perspective. Thus, for example, I do not refer to every article that supports my findings, nor do I refer to every article that reports failures to confirm my findings unless the failure challenges a fundamental aspect of my work. Third, it does not present new findings or theoretical developments; everything here (except as noted) has been published in peer-reviewed journals, or has been adapted from those publications.

So what is it? A story of how my ideas have developed, more or less chronologically, written as if I were explaining the ideas and data to attentive students. Thus, the text gets colloquial at times, and at other times it may be rather formal when the material is complex. I hope that it will provide some basic science background and a novel perspective for students and professionals who are applying behavioral principles to address socially significant problems.

Chapter 1 presents a review of basic concepts in the experimental analysis of behavior that figure in this book: Positive and negative reinforcement, response definition, stimulus control, and the concept of the discriminated operant. It also reviews basic response-reinforcer contingencies, schedules of reinforcement, Pavlovian contingencies, response strength, and resistance to change, all developed with reference to a 2004 study by Tim Shahan and Katie Burke that exemplifies many of these behavioral fundamentals. These topics should be familiar to readers who have taken undergraduate courses in learning and behavior analysis; advanced students and professionals may wish to argue with my way of presenting them.

Chapter 2 describes some standard research methods that are used in most of the studies discussed in this book, including the use of pigeons as experimental subjects. The chapter includes a sort of primer on the quantitative analyses involved, describing some simple mathematical functions and ways in which data may be transformed to evaluate how well they are described by those functions. The primer may be useful for students and others whose high-school algebra has become rusty.

Chapter 3 introduces early research on resistance to change that I published in 1974. The work grew out of a year as research associate at Harvard with Richard Herrnstein, who was developing a general formulation of choice and response rate that held for humans as well as nonhuman animals. His 1970 article was entitled "On the law of effect," and he construed his formulation as a law describing how reinforcement strengthens responding. In a related paradigm known as multiple schedules of reinforcement, my data showed that the rate of pigeons' discriminated operant behavior was generally higher and more resistant to change when a response was more frequently reinforced, consistent with Herrnstein's theory; but I argued that response strength should be identified with persistence or resistance to change rather than choice or response rate. Chapter 3 will also review related research on resistance to change with other species, including humans in laboratory and clinical settings.

Chapter 4 introduces the metaphor of behavioral momentum, which for me was a natural translation from classical physics to behavior. Newton's first and second laws of motion were taken as a metaphorical device to characterize behavior when an external variable is introduced, and a 1983 study with Charlotte Mandell and Jean Atak used the metaphor to quantify a behavioral equivalent of inertial mass. In 1997, Randy Grace and I devised a method for measuring preference between two conditions of reinforcement, as well as resistance to change, within individual subjects and experimental conditions, and found that these dependent variables were related by a simple equation that described the results of several separate experiments quite well. The approach was suggested by analogy to gravitational mass in Newton's Law of Gravitation; the convergence of results from different paradigms suggests that both resistance and preference are expressions of a single unifying construct that could be called strength, value, or behavioral mass.

Chapter 5 reviews a series of experiments by myself and others suggesting that free-operant response rate is determined by operant, response-reinforcer contingencies in accordance with Herrnstein's formulation, whereas resistance to change is determined independently by Pavlovian, stimulus-reinforcer contingencies. The results have been repeated with humans (and other species) in a variety of situations. A particularly challenging implication of these experiments is that a reinforcer-based intervention designed to reduce the rate of problem behavior in a clinical setting may also increase its persistence; some recent data illustrate this perverse implication.

Chapter 6 reviews experiments that challenge the major tenets of behavioral momentum theory, including multiple schedules with extremely different reinforcer rates in their components and single schedules of reinforcement where reinforcer rates are varied across conditions. I also consider several studies with equated reinforcer rates where high or low response rates are differentially reinforced in multiple-schedule components, or delays to reinforcement are introduced in one component. These studies challenge the Pavlovian interpretation of resistance to change in that differing stimulus-reinforcer relations are not necessary for differences in resistance to change. I consider a way of bringing these latter results into agreement with the general relation between resistance to change and preference described in Chapter 4.

Chapter 7 addresses the topic of resistance to extinction, especially the well-known finding that during extinction, response rate decreases more rapidly if every response has been reinforced than if responses were reinforced intermittently, according to some schedule of reinforcement. This so-called partial-reinforcement extinction effect (PREE) is exactly opposite to the basic predictions of momentum theory, a problem that I wrestled with for years. In 2000, Randy Grace and I proposed an equation that could solve the problem; in 2001, Ant McLean, Randy, and I confirmed its interpretation. I also review data on post-extinction recovery showing that extinction may not alter the effects of reinforcement on behavioral mass. Tim Shahan and his student Maggie Sweeney have extended the extinction model to account for relapse after apparently successful treatment of problem behavior when treatment is suspended.

Chapter 8 shows that the effects of reinforcement on accuracy in a discrimination task, and the resistance to change of accuracy, are strikingly similar to effects on the rate of a simple, repeatable response and its resistance to change. These findings grew out of a research collaboration with Amy Odum and Tim Shahan; Michael Davison participated in related theoretical developments. The theory and related findings suggest that attending to stimuli – a private process – can be reinforced; this may have implications for attentional problems in clinical and educational settings.

Chapter 9 describes some extrapolations of momentum concepts and basic research findings to the treatment of problem behavior in clinical settings, including a method for enhancing compliance with requests that has been called "behavioral momentum" and that has been highly effective in many settings. I will also discuss some current research that is exploring ways to circumvent problematic strengthening effects on problem behavior, and its subsequent tendency to relapse, that arise from treatments employing reinforcement of desirable alternative behavior.

A postscript will reflect on some implications of this rather mechanistic approach to behavior that is implicit in behavioral momentum theory. It will also extrapolate the concept of reinforcement, selection by consequences, and the momentum metaphor to one of the most pressing challenges of our time: Global warming and its consequences for the human future. I hope this extrapolation will encourage readers to use behavioral principles, including those developed in this book, to understand events in the world at large and to act on behalf of human wellbeing.

Chapter 1

Review of Basic Concepts

Clinical practitioners are often faced with the task of reducing or eliminating some form of problem behavior such as aggression, disruptive behavior, or self-injury. In many cases, the problem behavior has gone on for a long time and is extraordinarily resistant to treatment. People who engage in these sorts of activities are constant sources of concern for their families and teachers, are likely to be ostracized in schools or social settings, and may be consigned to institutional care with the attendant emotional, social, and monetary costs. Other sorts of problem behavior such as drug use or gambling can lead to the loss of an addict's job, family, and social standing; family members often suffer from deprivation or abuse; and the community or state gets stuck with the resulting costs. These are also problems for behavioral science: Why do people persist in courses of action that have such apparently negative consequences? And what can be done to help them to change their behavior, and to make desirable changes persist in the face of challenges or temptations?

This book will argue that some fundamental behavioral processes underlie the persistence of all behavior, whether it be harmful to the individual and society, such as drug addiction, or constructive and socially desirable, such as the dedicated pursuit, in the laboratory, of drugs that could cure Alzheimer's disease. In order to understand those fundamental processes, a lot of psychologists study the behavior of animal subjects in the laboratory, where their prior histories and current conditions can be controlled as precisely as one wishes. The assumption, in doing so, is that basic behavioral processes are common to all creatures – or at least to all vertebrates – that move about and interact with the natural environment. The basic processes identified in the laboratory are not the whole story, by a long shot. We know that the actions of animals – including human animals – are determined in part by their genetic endowments, which are given by natural selection. Humans also interact with each other via language, and of course human behavior is affected by social and cultural conditions. Genetics, language, and culture can combine with a subject's history and current circumstances in complex ways. But it is probably wise to begin with the simplest possible level of analysis: Study the behavior of individual animals under experimentally controlled conditions, compare the results with those of individual human subjects under comparable conditions, and then interpret human behavior in relatively uncontrolled social settings in the light of the processes revealed in the lab.

An experimental example

In 2004, Tim Shahan and Katie Burke, at Utah State University, reported some intriguing results of an experiment with rats that had been accustomed to drink a 10% solution of alcohol.[1] The rats were trained to press a lever that occasionally produced a drink in two alternating conditions, known as components of a multiple schedule. In one component, lever presses produced small alcoholic drinks from a dipper at unpredictable intervals averaging 15 seconds. In the other component, lever presses produced the same drinks at the same intervals but in addition, food pellets were given freely, regardless of what the rat was doing, also at unpredictable 15-second intervals. The two components were distinguished by tones and lights, and alternated frequently so that their effects on the rats' behavior could be compared within each experimental session. The point of this was to see if providing food as an alternative to the rewarding effects of alcohol would reduce responding that produced alcohol, and to find out how that alternative food might affect the persistence of responding for alcohol.

As anticipated on the basis of several previous studies (and common sense: why work when you can get something free), all rats pressed the alcohol-producing lever at a lower rate in the condition with added free food; thus, their tendency to seek a potentially addictive reward was reduced by having another sort of reward to consume in the same situation.

Now here's the intriguing result: When both alcohol and food deliveries were discontinued altogether, in both components, to evaluate the persistence of responding in the absence of any rewards, the rats responded more persistently and at higher rates in the component that had previously included free food. Thus, although the rate of alcohol-seeking was reduced by adding a free alternative reward, the persistence of alcohol-seeking was enhanced. The results are shown in Figure 1.1.

Although it used rats as subjects, the Shahan-Burke

15

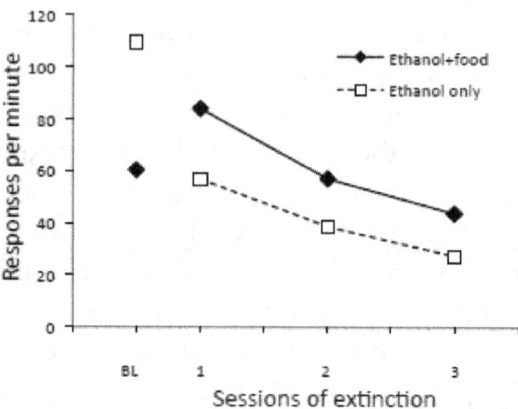

Figure 1.1. At the left, data points above BL display the average baseline response rates for four rats in two components of a multiple schedule as described in the text. During extinction, alcohol-seeking was more persistent in the presence of stimuli that had signaled added alternative reinforcers (replotted from data of Shahan & Burke, 2004).

experiment raises the possibility that alternative rewards may increase the persistence of attempts to engage in addictive drinking in humans as well. With humans, many therapy programs that are designed to deal with problem behavior arrange alternative rewards as a way to reduce that behavior. If those rewards also increase the persistence of problem behavior, it would be a nasty outcome of an otherwise good way to help people stop doing things that are bad for them and their families and communities.

Of course, there are lots of cases where persistence is valuable. For example, a therapist working with a couple in a troubled marriage might help them to communicate more effectively by prompting and guiding them through discussion of some difficult issues during an hour-long session in the therapist's office. The presumption is

16

that whatever the couple may learn in therapy will carry over into their daily lives and help them discuss stressful situations at home without accusation or anger. Indeed, therapy would be quite pointless if newly learned ways of behaving collapsed as soon as therapy sessions ended.

This book is concerned with the resistance to change of learned behavior that has been established by reinforcement in a distinctive stimulus situation. I have used the term "behavioral momentum" to characterize the tendency for behavior to keep on going, once it has been set into motion, despite disruptive changes in the subject's situation. I will review and interpret some findings of experiments on resistance to change in my laboratory and others, most of them with pigeons as subjects, and I will describe some parallel experiments with human subjects that have obtained similar results, with extensions to clinical and educational settings. But first, I will review some fundamental concepts, methods, and terminology in the science of behavior. This review is intended for readers whose background may be limited to a few undergraduate courses or general reading; more advanced students and professionals should skim, skip, or otherwise get directly to matters of central concern.

Reinforcement and the discriminated operant

The ABCs of behavior analysis, whether it be experimental or applied or purely conceptual, are Antecedents (stimuli), Behavior (responses), and Consequences (events that follow responses). The combination of a particular stimulus, a designated response, and a consequence that affects behavior is known as a discriminated operant. It is like an element of a story: A character enters a situation, acts on it, and then something happens; and the changed situation leads to some further action, with further consequences; and so forth.

Reinforcers

Behavioral momentum theory is concerned with the way in which the persistence of discriminated operant behavior is affected by reinforcement, which is probably the most frequently used term in the experimental analysis of behavior. As defined in most textbooks, reinforcement is the name for a process that involves both an experimental procedure and its effect. The procedure is to present an event following the occurrence of a response by an organism, and the effect is an increase in the probability of that response. That event is then identified as a reinforcer. Thus, "reinforcement" names a way to change behavior, but does not explain that change unless the experimenter knew in advance that the event was a reinforcer, independently of finding that it served to increase the probability of the behavior in question.

Behavioral research has not been able – at least not yet – to identify any single property that is common to all reinforcers and is absent for all non-reinforcers. Therefore, experimental analysis takes a pragmatic approach: If something has been an effective reinforcer in previous research, it will probably be an effective reinforcer in similar situations that have not yet been explored. In the Shahan-Burke experiment, for example, earlier studies in their and others' labs had shown that a 10% solution of alcohol could function as a reinforcer for rats, and the freely given food pellets that were presented in one condition have been used to reinforce responses like lever pressing in countless experiments and teaching laboratories beginning with B. F. Skinner's pioneering work in the 1930s.[2]

Reinforcers are usually classified as positive or negative. When something is presented after a response and the rate of responding increases, that something is called a positive reinforcer. In the classic laboratory example noted above, if a hungry rat presses a lever and a food pellet is dropped into an open dish – and if the rate of lever-pressing increases – food is a positive reinforcer. By contrast, when something is removed after a response and the rate of responding increases, that something is called a negative reinforcer. In the lab, if a mild electric shock is applied to a rat's feet, and is switched off when the rat presses a lever – and if the rat presses the lever sooner the next time it gets a shock – then shock is a negative reinforcer.

The same procedures and results can operate in daily life. For example, in a classroom, if a pupil turns in a perfect worksheet and is praised by the teacher – and if the pupil completes the next worksheet more rapidly – praise is a positive reinforcer. However, if the teacher repeatedly demands that the child hurry up and finish a worksheet, the child eventually complies, and the teacher stops making demands – and if the child then completes the next worksheet more rapidly – demands would exemplify negative reinforcement. Note that for both rat and child, the procedures defining positive and negative reinforcement differ but the outcomes are the same, at least with respect to lever pressing and worksheet completion. But note that the rat might try to escape from the experimental chamber associated with shock, and the child might avoid the classroom with the demanding teacher (or skip school altogether).

In real-world applied settings, there is so much variation between people and their histories – the back-story that each person brings to any situation – that reinforcers must often be identified individually. For example, attention might be effective with one child, playing electronic games with another, and watching TV with a third. Once an effective reinforcer is identified for an individual, though, it is likely to prove effective for several different responses and can be used to accomplish desirable changes in behavior.

Operants and response classes

Responses that are followed by reinforcers according to various contingencies (see below) are called operants, because they operate on the environment. In the laboratory, operants can be defined mechanically. For example, lever pressing by a rat is defined by the force and distance required to operate a switch that then registers "response" for the recording and control apparatus (usually a computer). The mechanical definition of the response is usually kept constant throughout an experiment. However, the topography of the response executed by the rat can take many forms – rapid or slow, forceful or gentle, with the left or right paw, and so forth, all with the same mechanical effect. Therefore, presenting food after an individual lever press is said to reinforce an instance of a response class called lever pressing, where successive instances may vary considerably but all variants that operate the switch are eligible for reinforcement.

In applied settings, the notion of a response class is

especially important: For example, aggressive responses by a person with mental retardation are defined not by a mechanical device but by an observer who records examples of hitting, biting, scratching, throwing objects, as so forth as instances of a class of activities that have something in common, such as violence directed toward another person.

Discriminative stimuli

Antecedent stimuli – physical events like lights or sounds – may have little or no impact on responding when they are first presented. But if a response is reinforced only while a particular light is on, responding will increase when the light is on and decrease when the light is off. The light is then known as a discriminative stimulus, and the process whereby it comes to affect behavior is known as discrimination or, more generally, stimulus control. The light can of course be described exactly in physical terms, but the effective discriminative stimulus may include a range of variations in the location or brightness of the light. For example, changing its brightness may or may not affect the rate of responding, depending on how much of a change is made, so the exact physical properties of the effective discriminative stimulus cannot be known a priori. Thus, "light on" is better thought of as the name of a stimulus class analogous to the response class named "lever pressing."

Compound stimuli raise another question. For example, the Shahan-Burke experiment used a pulsed tone and a flashing light as a discriminative stimulus to signal the availability of alcohol plus free food in one component, while the absence of tone and light served to signal alcohol only in the other component (these stimulus assignments were reversed for half of their rats). There is no way to know whether tone, light, or both were effective members of the stimulus classes distinguishing these components without performing separate tests. However, unless one is specifically interested in whether alcohol and food alter attending to tones versus lights, it does not matter: As long as stimulus control is demonstrated, the exact physical specification of the stimulus class is usually irrelevant.

In applied work with people who exhibit aggressive behavior, it is obviously important to identify the stimuli that evoke it: a particular classroom, or a particular teacher, or a request to perform a task. Once the effective stimuli are known, teachers and caregivers can try not to present stimuli that fall into the class of events that provoke violent attacks.

The notion that the discriminated operant involves classes of stimuli, responses, and reinforcers is extremely important for attempts to extend principles developed through controlled laboratory research to the more open and varied settings of schoolrooms and clinics in the real world. Unless the relevant classes can be identified with reasonable confidence, extrapolations from basic laboratory research can be meaningless – or worse, misleading. Therefore, efforts to use laboratory principles to address clinical, educational, or social problems are fraught with risk; but because the stakes are high, the risk is worth taking.

The discriminated operant provides a way to consider the general question of "what is learned" when a response is reinforced. So-called S-R theories of learning developed in the 1930s and 1940s suggested that a subject learns an association between the discriminative stimulus and the response, where the reinforcer strengthens the associative link. More recently, converging evidence from a variety of experiments has accumulated to suggest that the association includes the reinforcer (S^R) itself – that is, the reinforcer is a part of the learned relations involving stimuli and responses. Thus, the S-R-S^R compound is fundamental to associative learning theory, just as the ABC discriminated operant is the fundamental unit in experimental analyses. As suggested above, complete specification of the effective stimulus class, the operant class, and the effective reinforcer may not be known a priori. However, experimental analyses can proceed by holding constant the physical setting, the physical definition of the response, and the consequences of responding, and then varying one element at a time as required by the research question being addressed. For example, Shahan and Burke established two discriminated operants with alcohol reinforcers, one with added food pellets and one without, and later discontinued both alcohol and food – a procedure known as extinction – in order to compare the persistence of the two discriminated operants. Chapter 7 will consider ways to interpret persistence data when reinforcers are discontinued.

Contingencies of reinforcement

Above, I said that reinforcement involves the presentation of a reinforcing stimulus following a designated response. The meaning of "following" involves a sequential contingency, an *if-then* relation. The strongest possible response-reinforcer contingency is *if-and-only-if*: If the lever is pressed, then food is presented, and if no lever press, no

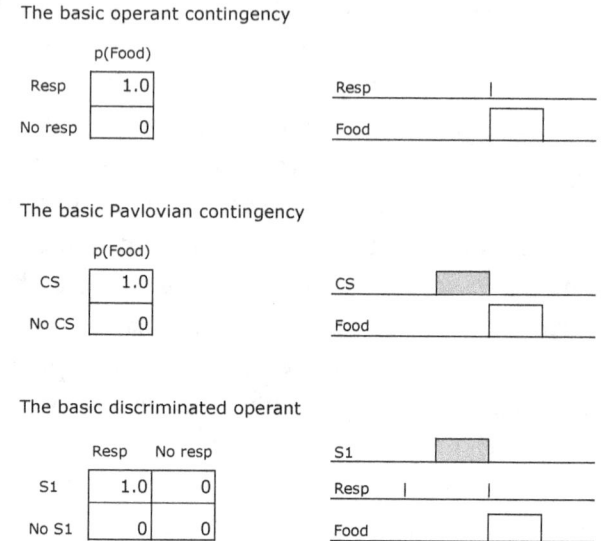

Figure 1.2. Diagrammatic representations of operant and Pavlovian contingencies in the top and middle panels. The squares at the left show the probability of food presentation. The diagrams at the right show the same relations in time, so that (for example) delays between responses and food, or the durations of the CS and/or intervals between CS and food can be displayed. The discriminated operant is represented as a 2x2 contingency in the bottom panel: A response produces food with probability 1.0 (in this example) only if a distinctive stimulus S1 is present.

food is presented. This maximal contingency is illustrated in the upper segment of Figure 1.2, both as a contingency square on the left and a time diagram on the right.

The response-reinforcer contingency may be weakened in either of two ways. First, food may also be presented occasionally when the rat is not engaged in lever pressing: If press, then food, and if no press, then food (sometimes). Second, food may be presented after some but not all lever presses: If press, then food (sometimes), if no press, then no food. And of course the contingency can be relaxed in both ways: If press, then food (sometimes); if no press, then food (sometimes). Schedules of reinforcement (see below) make "sometimes" explicit.

Pavlovian conditioning and contingencies

Response independence is the procedural hallmark of Pavlovian conditioning. The classic example comes from Pavlov's extensive work with salivary responses in dogs.[3] Food in the mouth (the unconditional stimulus, US, equivalent to a reinforcer) elicits salivation in an obligatory reflexive fashion (the unconditional response, UR). And as every student knows, the dog will salivate (the conditional response, CR) when a bell rings (the conditional stimulus, CS) if the bell has preceded food presentation on a number of occasions (called trials). But the dog is not required to salivate in order to obtain food: The procedure involves a contingent relation between stimuli and reinforcers, rather than between responses and reinforcers as in operant contingencies.

The strongest possible stimulus-reinforcer contingency is: if bell, then food; if no bell, then no food, regardless of whether salivation occurs or not. This maximal contingency is illustrated in Figure 1.2, middle panel, paralleling the illustration of operant contingencies above. There are two ways to weaken the stimulus-reinforcer contingency that are analogous to weakening the response-reinforcer contingency. First, food may also be given in the absence of the bell: if bell, then food; if no bell, then food at some other time. And second, food may be withheld after some bell-rings: If bell, then food (sometimes), if no bell, then no food. Here, the "sometimes" is usually given by the probability of food on a trial, defining various degrees of so-called partial reinforcement. Again, these two ways to weaken the contingency can be combined, so that not all CS presentations include the reinforcer, and reinforcers are presented at random times when the CS is absent.

It is important to note that discriminated operant contingencies, shown in the bottom panel of Figure 1.2, entail implicit Pavlovian contingencies. For example, if an experiment arranges that lever pressing is reinforced when a light is on, but not when the light is off, there is an implicit light-food contingency as well as a lever press-food contingency. Thus, in the Shahan-Burke experiment, there is a more favorable stimulus-reinforcer contingency in the alcohol-plus-food condition than in the alcohol-only condition.

Implicit operant contingencies may also lurk within Pavlovian contingencies: in the classic Pavlovian bell-food experiment, there is an implicit operant contingency if anticipatory salivation makes the food taste better. Partly for these reasons, some learning theorists have suggested that operant and Pavlovian conditioning are fundamentally the same despite the differences in experimentally arranged contingencies. I won't go into the theoretical arguments here, but the Pavlovian stimulus-reinforcer contingencies implicit in the discriminated operant will be central to some analyses of resistance to change that will be discussed in Chapter 5.

Although not specifically included in the logic of contingency, time is obviously important. Operant response-reinforcer contingencies where food is presented immediately after a lever press are much more effective in increasing response rate than logically identical contingencies where food follows a lever press after, say, 30 seconds – although even with such long delays, rats eventually learn to press a lever. Likewise, Pavlovian conditioning proceeds most rapidly when the US follows the CS by a second or two – although, again, conditioning of some sorts of responses can occur with much longer CS-US delays. Thus, time is a parameter of contingent relations between events and should be included in the description of contingencies as in the time diagrams in Figure 1.2. For example, an operant contingency might be specified as: if lever press, then food after 30 s; if no lever press, then no food. To weaken such a contingency, one could present food every 60 s in the absence of lever pressing. The same can be done in Pavlovian conditioning with widely spaced trials: If bell, then food after 30 s; if no bell, then food every 60 s. In general, both operant and Pavlovian conditioning are most effective with strong contingencies and short delays separating the critical events.

Schedules of reinforcement

Contingencies of reinforcement for operant behavior include rules for the scheduling of reinforcers with respect to time and responses. For example, if food is given after some number of lever presses (a ratio schedule), the usual result is a high rate of responding. If the number of required responses is the same for each successive reinforcer, the schedule is known as *fixed ratio* (FR) and pauses in responding usually occur after each reinforcer, followed by a high rate until the next reinforcer is presented. By contrast, if the number of required responses varies unpredictably from one reinforcer to the next, the schedule is known as *variable ratio* (VR) and response rate is usually high and free of pauses throughout periods between reinforcers.

An interval schedule is defined if food is given after the first lever press to occur following the passage of some time. If the time between reinforcers is constant, the schedule is designated *fixed interval* (FI) and the usual result is a pause after each reinforcer followed by a moderate rate of responding until the next reinforcer is presented. If the time between reinforcers varies unpredictably from one reinforcer to the next, the schedule is designated *variable interval* (VI), and response rate is usually moderate and steady throughout periods between reinforcers. [The Shahan-Burke experiment used a variant of VI schedules called random-interval (RI) schedules that make reinforcement available with constant probability in time.] With either VI or RI schedules, the number of reinforcers obtained by lever pressing would be about the same for the high and low baseline response rates in the two components.

Stylized versions of performances on FI, FR, VI, and VR schedules are presented as cumulative records in Figure 1.3, which show how the cumulative total of responses increases in relation to time within an experimental session (the total cannot decrease even if response rate falls to zero).

The passage of time is represented on the *x*-axis, and the total number of responses emitted up to that time is displayed on the *y*-axis. A horizontal line signifies no responding at all, and a steep upward line signifies a high rate of responding. Thus, on the FR schedule, each reinforcer is followed by a period without responding (known as the post-reinforcement pause) represented as a horizontal line, after which there is an fairly abrupt

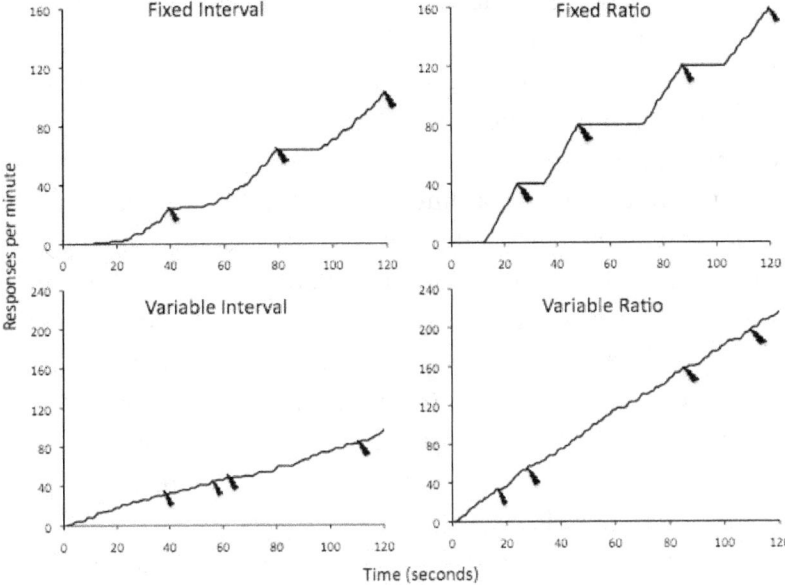

Figure 1.3. Stylized representations of typical cumulative records of responding on classical schedules of reinforcement; reinforcers are indicated as downward blips. Scales of y-axes differ for fixed (upper panels) and variable schedules (lower panels). Note that the pause-after-reinforcement-then-respond pattern is similar for FI and FR schedules, and that response rates are roughly constant over time between reinforcers for VI and VR schedules.

transition to a high response rate, represented as a steep upward-sloping line, that continues until a reinforcer is obtained. A similar pattern arises in FI schedules, but the transition to responding may be less abrupt.

Although the temporal patterns of responding are similar on FR and FI schedules, and on VR and VI schedules, response rates are lower on interval schedules than on ratio schedules even when the numbers and temporal patterns of reinforcers actually obtained during

29

a defined period are the same. Intuitively, it makes sense to respond faster on ratio schedules because doing so increases the obtained rate of reinforcement; experimental analyses have suggested that other factors may also operate. However, the detailed processes responsible for the difference in responding maintained by interval and ratio schedules may not be critical for resistance to change, the topic of fundamental interest here.

Another sort of contingency that directly determines the rate of responding is differential reinforcement of only those responses that meet a temporal criterion. For example, a response may be reinforced only after the lapse of some number of seconds since a previous response (known as DRL, for *differential reinforcement of low rate*). Or a response may be reinforced only if some number of previous responses have occurred within a brief time (known as DRH, for *differential reinforcement of high rate*). Not surprisingly, DRL and DRH schedules produce response rates more or less in accord with the temporal contingencies they arrange. There are many different ways to combine schedules and contingencies of these sorts, with correspondingly different operant performances; a substantial book by Charles Ferster and B. F. Skinner, published in 1957, was devoted to the topic.

The presentation of a reinforcer in the absence of a response may also be scheduled. For example, food may be presented only if no lever press has occurred for some number of seconds (known as DRO, for *differential reinforcement of other behavior*). Finally, reinforcers may be presented at random times regardless of responding. This is known as response-independent or noncontingent reinforcement according to a *variable-time* (VT) schedule.

DRO contingencies usually produce near-zero response rates, whereas responding on VT schedules can be quite variable, depending in part on whether responses happen by chance to coincide with reinforcers, known as adventitious reinforcement. Shahan and Burke used a random-time (RT) schedule, which is essentially the same as a VT schedule, to present food pellets in the alcohol-plus-free-pellets condition, and lever presses may have been reinforced adventitiously by food in addition to experimentally arranged reinforcement by alcohol. However, if lever pressing had been adventitiously reinforced in the alcohol-plus-free-pellets condition, its rate should have been higher, whereas in fact it was lower; but whenever reinforcers are presented independently of responding, their effect on ongoing behavior is likely to depend on the nature of the behavior, the reinforcer, and the frequency of their adventitious co-occurrence in time.

Resistance to extinction

My basic concern is the resistance to change of discriminated operant behavior. Perhaps the most common method for evaluating resistance to change is extinction, which is the name for both an experimental operation: withholding a previously given reinforcer; and a result: the subsequent decrease in responding. As we have seen, Shahan and Burke used extinction as a method to compare the persistence of alcohol-reinforced lever-pressing in components with and without added free food, and observed greater resistance to extinction in the component that had included free food.

There must be several thousand published studies of resistance to extinction, most of them designed to evaluate various theoretical interpretations of the extinction process, but the primary interest here is that extinction is one method among many to challenge behavior that has been established by reinforcement. The following chapters will consider several other methods for evaluating resistance to change that do not involve discontinuing reinforcement. One reason for exploring challenges other than extinction is that the experimental analysis of behavior has long served as a source of methods and principles for applied work in clinics, institutions, schools, and daily life. Applied psychologists and teachers must be concerned with ways to increase resistance to change because establishing some desirable behavior in the clinic or classroom is of little value unless that new behavior persists through the various distractions and disruptions of daily life. And applied workers must be especially interested in new behavior that is naturally reinforced in everyday interactions, such as helping others. Resistance to extinction is of great interest as a behavioral process, but it would be pointless to establish some new behavior that would never be reinforced — thus, by definition, would not be desirable — in the real world.

Response strength and resistance to change

For better or worse, my initial interest in resistance to change arose not from a desire to help behavioral therapists and teachers, but from the connotations of "reinforcement" in everyday language and their implications for basic research. Reinforcing a concrete structure makes it more resistant to collapse in an earthquake, so by analogy, reinforcing a response in a given stimulus situation makes the discriminated operant more resistant to some challenge that tends to disrupt ongoing behavior. Whether this is a legitimate implication of the term "reinforcement" or not, the sheer persistence of behavior – including both desirable and problem behavior occurring in real-world settings – is interesting and important in its own right.

Another reason for my concern with resistance to change derives from the closely related notion of response strength. In 1938, Skinner suggested that reinforcement strengthens responding in the sense of increasing its probability of occurrence in time. Therefore, he proposed that the rate of a freely occurring response was the appropriate measure of its strength. In everyday language, though, strength has other connotations. To use the example above, a building is said to be strong if it stands up during an earthquake. By analogy, the strengthening effect of reinforcement on discriminated operant behavior may best be measured by its resistance to some equivalent of an earthquake – an external disruptive event imposed during ongoing behavior.

In 1974, just as I was preparing a journal article reporting some studies of resistance to change of key pecking in pigeons (see Chapter 3), Kendon Smith published a theoretical article arguing that the effectiveness of reinforcement in increasing the rate of a response could be measured by the magnitude of some operation such as punishment that exactly cancels reinforcement and reduces response rate to zero.[4] His well-reasoned article supports my argument from everyday usage: reinforcement, response strength, and resistance to change are inextricably linked in the study of learned behavior.

Chapter 2

Research Methods and Measures

There are some aspects of research methods that are general to most of the experiments discussed in the following chapters and I'd like to get them out of the way here.

Experimental subjects, responses, and measures

Although I used rats and lever pressing as examples in the preceding chapter, most of the experiments considered here have used pigeons as subjects and key pecking as the response, for practical as well as scientific reasons. Pigeons are relatively cheap to breed or to buy and then to house, feed, and maintain in good health for many years. In the laboratory, pigeons live in fairly spacious cages, with water and pigeon grit (which they use to grind up grain in their crops) always available. Before and during an experiment, the birds are deprived of food in order to make food an effective reinforcer, and maintained at 80-85% of the weights they would attain if given continuous free access to food. (Before getting exercised about the harshness of this deprivation regime, the reader should consider what a person's free-feeding body weight might be if he or she were left alone in an apartment with a well-stocked fridge and nothing to do but eat. Most of us are probably somewhere near 80% of that weight and all the healthier as a result.) There is no evidence that a pigeon's health is adversely affected by restricted feeding of this sort. Under these conditions, many of my pigeons have lived for 15 to 20 years, so an experiment that takes a year or more occupies a modest fraction of an adult bird's life. (By comparison, a year-long experiment with a rat would take it from young adulthood to old age.)

Another reason for using pigeons is that the apparatus for research on operant behavior with this species – a roughly cubic chamber with a houselight for general illumination, back-lighted translucent keys on one wall that send electrical signals to recording and control equipment when pecked, and a grain feeder below the keys – is quite similar from one laboratory to another, so it is relatively easy to compare results. Moreover, it's fairly easy to train pigeons to peck lighted keys for grain, and their rate of sustained key pecking can range up to 200-300 pecks per minute, a really wide dynamic range for study. So my colleagues and I have used pigeons, rate of key pecking, and grain reinforcement in the majority of our research, and many related studies by other researchers have done likewise.

The choice of key-pecking rate as the dependent variable derives from B. F. Skinner's early identification of response rate with response strength: When a response was reinforced, the higher the rate, the stronger the response. Relatedly, a natural choice for the independent variable is the rate of reinforcement: If reinforcement strengthens responding, then the more frequently a response is reinforced, the stronger it should be. Early studies by Richard Herrnstein and his students at Harvard, and by Nat Schoenfeld and his students (including me) at Columbia, had shown that the rate of reinforcement was an important determiner of response rate – at least as important as, say, the magnitude of the reinforcer. If ratio schedules are used (see Chapter 1), reinforcer rate is directly proportional to response rate because the faster the bird pecks, the sooner it gets grain. Thus, the independent and dependent variables are perfectly confounded. However, if variable-interval (VI) schedules are arranged as described in Chapter 1, the pigeon's rate of key pecking can vary a lot without much effect on the obtained reinforcer rate. For example, a VI 1-minute schedule will yield an a maximum of 60 reinforcers per hour no matter how rapidly a pigeon pecks, and even if the bird pecks fairly slowly, it will still pick up nearly all of the reinforcers that the schedule makes available in the course of an experimental session. So VI schedules are well (if not perfectly) suited to arranging reinforcer rate as an independent variable, and for that reason have been used in most of the studies to be described in the following chapters.

Behavioral experiments with pigeons, rats, or other creatures are usually conducted in daily sessions, run at about the same time of day so that the results are not affected by diurnal variations in the subject's level of activity or appetite. Typically, sessions are about an hour long, and the experiment is often designed so that the subject can obtain enough food reinforcers to maintain it near 80-85% of its free-feeding weight; if reinforcers are too infrequent, the subject gets supplemental feeding in its home cage.

Shaping and autoshaping

Before an experiment begins, there is usually some preliminary training that gets the subject accustomed to the experimental chamber, where it receives noncontingent reinforcers ("magazine training") until it consumes them readily. Then the subject is trained to make the response that will be measured. For a rat, training is not always needed. For example, after magazine training, a rat often presses a lever while moving around the chamber, receives a food pellet, and before long presses the lever again and gets another pellet. After a few minutes and a few more presses and pellets, the rat usually presses the lever consistently. But sometimes the rat doesn't touch the lever and the response must be shaped by hand – almost literally molded, as by a sculptor. The experimenter watches the rat and takes advantage of seemingly random variations in its movements. For example, food might be presented only if the rat is near the lever in the course of exploring the chamber. Then, when the rat is hanging out in the vicinity of the lever, food is presented only when it is facing the lever, then only when it lifts a paw, then only when the paw moves toward the lever, and then only when the paw touches and presses the lever. The shaping process is technically known as "selective reinforcement of successive approximations," and it is great fun to shape complex, amusing performances like picking up a marble and dropping it into a cup.

Shaping a pigeon's key peck by hand involves the same sort of approach, but it is often more convenient to use a method called "autoshaping." The method was introduced by Paul Brown and Herbert Jenkins, not as a methodological convenience but as a novel and important behavioral process that must be appreciated in relation to some experiments that will be discussed in subsequent chapters.[1] Autoshaping arranges that the pecking key is lighted for a few seconds, with its offset followed immediately by food – a Pavlovian stimulus-reinforcer contingency (see Chapter 1). Outside the lab, pigeons peck at the ground to get their food, and in the lab, they peck at the grain feeder when it is presented. After a few trials with key light followed by food, pigeons usually peck at the key – a result that looks strikingly like Pavlovian conditioning where the CS is key light, the US is food, the UR is pecking-at-food, and the CR is pecking-at-CS-on-key. In effect, Brown and Jenkins showed that directed movement of the pigeon's head – usually construed as operant behavior – could be conditioned in Pavlovian fashion, and autoshaped key pecking has been used extensively in subsequent research on the principles of Pavlovian conditioning. However, the pigeon's key peck also has the properties of an operant, in that its rate of occurrence is readily changed by operant contingencies of the sort embodied in schedules of reinforcement. This duality of the pigeon's peck has occasioned a complicated literature, but for our purposes it is enough to appreciate that pecking can be established and maintained by Pavlovian stimulus-reinforcer contingencies, and that this may complicate the interpretation of operant response-reinforcer contingencies in evaluations of resistance to change.

From acquisition to the steady state

Once lever pressing or key pecking is established, the automatic apparatus can take over and the first phase of the experiment proper – known as acquisition – can begin, and the subject's rate of responding typically increases over successive daily sessions. The psychology of learning is especially concerned with acquisition, especially in Pavlovian conditioning where the experimenter can control the presentation of stimuli and reinforcers regardless of what the subject does. For example, in autoshaping, the number of trials required for pigeons to peck a key on 9 out of 10 trials may be examined in relation to the probability that food follows key light, the duration of the key light, the intertrial interval between keylight presentations, and the like, in order to determine how the rapidity of learning depends on temporal and reinforcement variables.

Experiments of this sort necessarily make comparisons between groups of subjects because once a subject has acquired some performance, it cannot de-acquire and re-acquire it under different conditions. In research with independent groups, all members of each group must have similar histories (or preferably, be naïve with respect to the stimuli, responses, and reinforcers involved) before the study begins. The groups' acquisition data may then be compared statistically. Textbooks of research methods and statistics describe various ways to do this, but I won't pursue them here because all comparisons of data discussed in this book are based on individual subjects studied within or between experimental conditions.

Virtually all of the basic research discussed here concerns the effects of reinforcement on behavior long after acquisition is complete – that is, after response rate reaches a stable level that is repeatable from one session to the next, often called "steady-state" behavior.

Conducting daily sessions and examining the data for stability can be pretty tedious, and even after stability is finally achieved, it may take many more sessions with different conditions of reinforcement to answer interesting questions. For example, to determine how the rate of responding depends on the rate of reinforcement, an experimenter might arrange different variable-interval (VI) schedules in successive conditions, keeping each condition in effect for enough sessions to permit response rate to stabilize at a new value. After determining stable response rates at different reinforcer rates over a wide range, the experimenter should repeat at least one previous determination to see whether subsequent experience has altered the response rate obtained at a reinforcer rate that was in effect perhaps months earlier. Boring. But finally, after a year or so, the researcher can construct a graph relating response rate to reinforcer rate, compare it with results for other species, responses, and reinforcers, try to describe it with a mathematical equation, and perhaps identify a quantitative law of behavior. And that's exciting. As Donald Lewis pointed out in an early textbook on quantitative methods, "The highest level of scientific description is represented by precise statements of relationships between two or more variables under specified conditions. The most unequivocal and most universally understood of such statements are those set down as mathematical functions."[2]

Algebraic functions and logarithmic transforms

There are some simple functions in this book, none of them requiring more background than high-school algebra. Here's a refresher.

The simplest expression relating some aspect of behavior y to some experimental variable x is linear:

$$y = a + bx.$$

(2.1)

If $x = 0$, a is the y-intercept of Equation 2.1. If $a = 0$, y is directly proportional to x, where b is the constant of proportionality – the slope of the function on a graph of y vs x. Figure 2.1 displays a graph of a linear increasing function with $a = 2.0$ and $b = 0.6$, together with hyperbolic, exponential, and power functions described in the next few paragraphs.

Equation 2.1 is a potential candidate for describing the relation between response rate and reinforcer rate, where a would represent the rate in the absence of any experimentally arranged reinforcement, known as operant level, and b would characterize the amount by which response rate increased for each unit increase in reinforcer rate. However, Equation 2.1 states that y will increase without limit as x becomes indefinitely large, whereas response rate is limited by the mechanics of the response itself. For example, a rat can press a lever only once or twice per second because the lever must be released before the next press can be recorded, and this takes some time. Therefore, a realistic descriptive function must have an upper limit known as its asymptote. One candidate, which we will encounter in Chapter 3, is the hyperbolic function:

$$y = \frac{bx}{x + a}.$$

(2.2)

If $x = 0$, $y = 0$, and if $a = 0$, then $y = b$ – i.e., there

41

is no effect of x. But if a is constant and greater than 0, y increases as x increases but at a decreasing rate, and as x becomes very large, $x/(x+a)$ approaches 1.0, so b is the asymptote of Equation 2.2. If the value of a is equal to x, the value of y is one-half of the asymptoptic value b. Accordingly, a is sometimes known as the "half-life" of the hyperbola and quantifies the rate at which y approaches the asymptote. For the function shown in Figure 2.1, $a = 4$ and $b = 16$. More generally, the hyperbola characterizes the apparent effect of diminishing returns on investment: When your savings are small, adding a few dollars makes a big subjective difference in the value of your account, but as the account grows, adding that same number of dollars seems to make less and less difference.

Another function that has desirable properties is the exponential,

$$y = a^x. \qquad (2.3)$$

If a is greater than 1.0, the function increases without limit as x increases (this is how compound interest works, where a is 1.0 plus the annual interest rate and x is years). If a is less than 1.0, the function decreases and approaches 0 as its asymptote. This is how radioactivity decreases over time; below, we will compare the decreasing exponential with a version of the hyperbolic (Eq. 2.2), both of which have been used to describe short-term memory loss over time.

To make the exponential useful for describing data that increase at a decreasing rate and approach an asymptote from below, like Equation 2.2, one can express the difference between asymptote and the value of y as:

$$y = b(1 - a^x) \qquad (2.4)$$

If $x = 0$, the term $(1-a^x)$ equals 0 (because any number raised to the 0th power is 1; see below), so $y = 0$. Then, if a is less than 1.0, the term $(1-a^x)$ approaches 1.0 as x increases, so y approaches its asymptote b with a deviation from asymptote that decreases exponentially. For the function shown in Figure 2.1, $a = 0.8$ and $b = 14$. A nifty property of Equation 2.4 is that for each increase in x, y increases by a constant fraction of the difference between its current value and the asymptote. Equation 2.4 has often been used to describe the acquisition of a novel task, where y represents performance and x represents successive learning trials.

Exponential functions involve a constant a raised to a variable power x, and may be confused with power functions that involve a variable x raised to a constant power a. The power function is written:

$$y = bx^a \qquad (2.5)$$

If $x = 0$, $y = 0$. If $a = 0$, $y = b$ (i.e., x has no effect on y), and if $a = 1$, the function is linear, with y directly proportional to x. Values of x between 0 and 1 generate increasing, negatively accelerated functions that resemble increasing hyperbolic and exponential functions except that power functions increase without limit – i.e., there is no asymptote. For the function shown in Figure 2.1, $a = 0.5$ and $b = 3$. Power functions have been used to describe data in many domains of science; in psychology, they are often used to characterize the relation between judged sensory

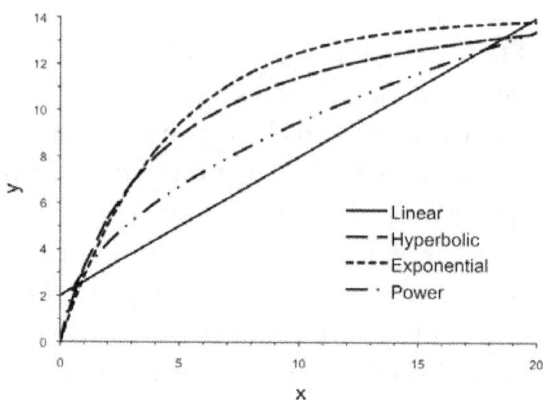

Figure 2.1. A comparison of linear, hyperbolic, exponential, and power functions given by Equations 2.1, 2.2, 2.4, and 2.5 with the values of parameters *a* and *b* given in the text.

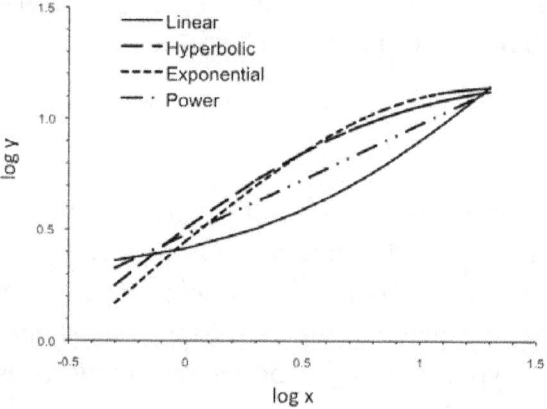

Figure 2.2. A comparison of linear, hyperbolic, exponential, and power functions given by Equations 2.1, 2.2, 2.4, and 2.5 and shown in Figure 2.1 with the values of *x* and *y* transformed to logarithms.

44

magnitudes and physical intensities of stimuli on many different continua.

It is often helpful to compare functions when values of x and y are transformed to logarithms. Figure 2.2 shows how the increasing linear, hyperbolic, exponential, and power functions in Figure 2.1 appear in log-log plots. The linear function becomes positively accelerated, the hyperbolic and exponential are negatively accelerated, and the power function is linear. Let's take a detour into the properties of logarithms in order to get an intuitive feeling for how they work.

The logarithm of any number is the power to which a standard, termed the base, must be raised to yield that number. For example, the logarithm to the base 10 (abbreviated $\log_{10}$) of 1000 is 3, because $10^3 = 1000$. As further examples, $\log_{10}$ of 100 is 2; $\log_{10}$ of 10 is 1; and $\log_{10}$ of 1 is 0, because any number raised to the 0th power is 1. To continue, $\log_{10}$ of 0.1 is -1; $\log_{10}$ of 0.01 is -2; and $\log_{10}$ of 0.001 is -3. Negative logarithms of positive fractional numbers arise because negative exponents signify reciprocals: for example, $10^{-2} = 1/10^2 = 1/100$.

To see that logarithms have the property of transforming equal ratios into equal differences, consider Table 2.1, presenting series of numbers differing by a factor of 10. Note especially that the logarithm of 1 is 0, and that logarithms are negative for numbers smaller than 1. However, the logarithms of 0 or of negative numbers are undefined, which is not a problem for the sorts of research on behavior considered here because all nonzero measures of behavior are positive. Note also that as numbers decrease and approach zero, their logarithms decrease without limit. This property of logarithms prevents them from encountering floor effects – i.e., the compression of their range as numbers approach zero.

Finally, a few simple rules for operating with logarithms. First, the logarithm of a product of two numbers equals the sum of the logarithms of those numbers: thus, $\log(10*100) = \log(10) + \log(100) = 3$. Second, the logarithm of a ratio of two numbers equals the difference between the logarithms of those numbers: for example, $\log(10/100) = \log(10) - \log(100) = -1$. Third, the logarithm of a number raised to a power equals the product of the power and the logarithm of the number. For example, $\log(10^3) = 3*\log(10) = 3$. And fourth, if you know the value of the logarithm of a number, you can obtain the value of that number by raising the base to the power of the log value. For example, if $\log_{10}(x) = 3$, $x = 10^3$. This process is called exponentiating or, less commonly, taking antilogs. All of these rules follow directly from the list of numbers and their logarithms in Table 2.1. To be sure of mastery, the reader should confirm these rules with other numbers, not the power-of-ten set that I used here for ease of understanding.

Logarithms are used extensively in mathematical descriptions of behavioral data because they transform equal ratios into equal intervals, as illustrated above where each ten-fold increase in a number is equivalent to a 1-unit increase in its logarithm. Although base-10 or "common" logarithms are often used because of our decimal system of numbers, and will be used throughout this book, mathematical analyses generally use logarithms to the base e, termed "natural" logarithms and abbreviated ln. Regardless of their base, logarithms always transform equal ratios into equal intervals.

Table 2.1. Illustration of some properties of logarithms

Number	Common logarithm
10,000	4
1,000	3
100	2
10	1
1	0
0.1	-1
0.01	-2
0.001	-3
0.0001	-4

In the following chapters, there will be several examples of graphs showing how response rate decreases when something is done to disrupt performance while the reinforcer rate is constant. The decreasing exponential presented above, $y = ba^x$, provides a way to describe such data with $a < 1.0$; b is the y-intercept when $x = 0$ (I've invented some for illustrative purposes in the upper panel of Figure 2.3). However, there are several other decreasing functions that look similar to the exponential, and it isn't always obvious that one or another is the best descriptor. The decreasing hyperbolic,

$$y = \frac{ba}{x+a},$$
  2.6

resembles the exponential in that it decreases from its y-intercept, b, when $x = 0$, to 0 as x becomes very large.

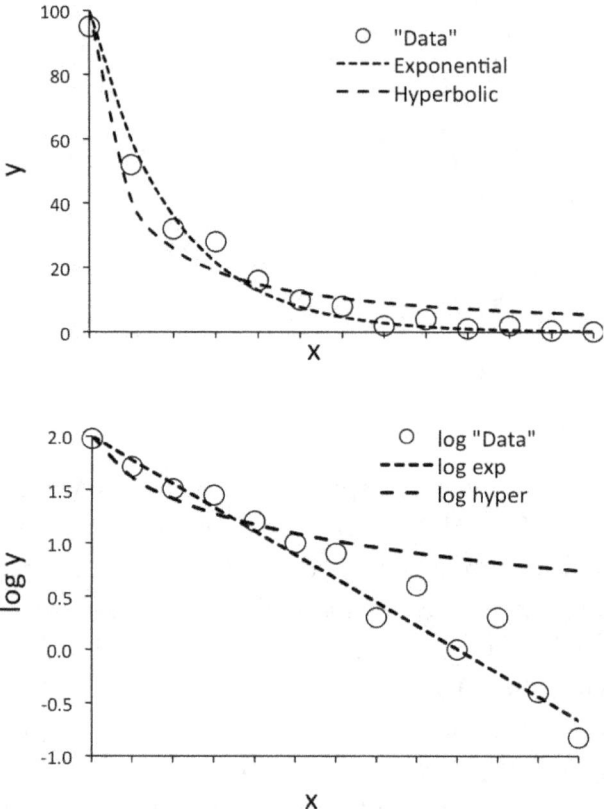

Figure 2.3. The upper panel presents some hypothetical data that might be described by exponential or hyperbolic decreasing functions, and the lower panel shows that when the data and predictions of these two equations are expressed as logarithms, the data appear to deviate somewhat less from the linear relation between log(y) and x predicted by the exponential.

When $x = a$, y = 0.5 b, so a is the half-life of the function. Both exponential and hyperbolic functions, with values of a chosen to give reasonable descriptions of the data, and also shown.

One way to distinguish the exponential and hyperbolic is to transform the data into logarithms, and also express the values predicted by these functions as logarithms (as in Figure 2.2). The exponential predicts a linear decreasing function when transformed to logarithms following the rules above:

$$\log(y) = \log(b) + \log(a)x .$$ (2.7)

Thus, the resulting graph is linear with slope equal to $\log(a)$ and intercept equal to $\log(b)$, as shown in the lower panel of Figure 2.3; I chose the value of $a = 0.6$ [$\log(a)$ = -0.22] and $b = 100$ [$\log(b)$ = 2.0] to give respectable agreement, by inspection, between the exponential function and the data.

The values of $\log y$ predicted by the hyperbolic are also shown in the lower panel of Figure 2.3; I chose the value of $a = 0.65$ to make the hyperbolic do about as well as the exponential for the upper left data points. However, the predictions clearly diverge as the value of x increases, and at least for these data, the exponential looks like a better descriptor.

Although visual inspection is important, a less subjective method is to ask your computer to choose the best-fitting exponential by adjusting the values of a and b so as to minimize the sum of squared differences between the data and the values given by the equation. Then repeat the process with the hyperbolic, and for descriptive purposes, use whichever function accounts best for the data. One function or another may be preferred for theoretical reasons, but that question goes beyond the topics of this chapter.

The constants *a* and *b* in the equations we have considered are known as its *parameters*, and their fitted values are higher-order dependent variables that can characterize an entire data set. For example, if the hypothetical experiment that yielded these data were repeated with (say) larger reinforcers, the effects of x might differ, and if the new data also looked reasonable in a graph of $\log y$ against x, the data of both experiments could be summarized by the fitted values of *a* and *b*.

It is essential that any equation used to describe data be compared with the data of individual subjects. The reason is that combining data across cases that differ in a simple quantitative way can lead to a qualitatively different (and incorrect) conclusion. To pursue the relation between pigeons' response rates and the experimentally arranged reinforcer rate, suppose that the response rates of all pigeons are two-valued: Up to some critical reinforcer rate, they peck at some low rate, and at all higher reinforcer rates they peck at some other, higher rate. Thus, the true relation between key pecking rate and reinforcer rate is a step function. But if that critical reinforcer rate and the low and high response rates below and above it vary randomly across birds, averaging their response rates at each reinforcer rate will produce a smooth increasing function of the sort portrayed in Figure 2.1 that does not even come close to representing the behavior of any individual.

In the interest of economy, I am going to present average data in the material that follows but only when they are representative of all individual subjects in an experiment. Complete individual data are given in many of the published research articles cited in the following chapters so readers can check my descriptions and conclusions for themselves.[3]

Why pigeons?

I couldn't begin to count the number of times that I have been challenged to demonstrate that studying pigeons pecking keys can teach us something useful about human behavior. Unless people are locked up in little rooms with nothing else to do or to eat, they don't bang on keys in order to get grain. But I will argue that pigeons and people do behave in functionally similar ways in experiments where comparable contingencies can be arranged, and I sometimes challenge audiences to tell me which of two data sets came from pigeons or from people. In each chapter, I will present some human examples that are related to my theme after describing the pigeon results, and will argue that the principles identified in experimental research can be extrapolated, with suitable caution, to humanly important clinical, educational, and social settings. In particular, the principles of behavioral momentum developed in the pigeon lab can help us to understand the tendency for individuals to persist in both beneficial and destructive activities. Speculatively, the same principles may also help us to understand humans' propensity to destroy their own environments, and perhaps to alter the grim future that awaits humankind if that propensity goes unchecked.

Chapter 3

Choice, Response Rate, and Resistance to Change

The quantitative methods summarized in Chapter 2 became prominent in experimental analyses of operant behavior during the 1960s. Interestingly, an early and algebraically simple application arose from an experimental complication: offering pigeons a choice between two adjacent response keys rather than arranging a single defined operant. Either key could be pecked at any time throughout the course of an experimental session, and food reinforcers were arranged separately for each response by two independent variable-interval (VI) schedules. The arrangement is known as free-operant concurrent schedules. Although this procedure had been employed by several researchers, including B. F. Skinner, who described it in his 1950 article "Are theories of learning necessary?" Richard Herrnstein was the first to arrange systematic variations in the reinforcer rates for both responses and to present a mathematical description of the results.[1]

Concurrent schedules

Herrnstein's data were strikingly orderly: The

proportion of pecks to one key roughly equaled the proportion of reinforcers obtained from that key. This result may be written as an equation known as the *matching law*.

$$\frac{B_1}{B_1 + B_2} = \frac{r_1}{r_1 + r_2}.$$

(3.1)

In this equation, B_1 and B_2 are the numbers of pecks to alternatives 1 and 2, and r_1 and r_2 are the numbers of reinforcers obtained from those alternatives. The equal sign asserts that behavior proportions match reinforcer proportions. Equation 3.1 is illustrated with hypothetical data in Figure 3.1. Similar real data have been obtained with humans, monkeys, rats, and other nonhuman animals as well as pigeons. Because the matching relation is simple, general, and quantitative, Equation 3.1 deserves its designation as a law of behavior.

I was a visiting research fellow at Harvard in 1966-67 and was caught up in the excitement of ongoing experimental and quantitative developments. Every week at the "pigeon meetings," Herrnstein and his graduate students presented the latest results of experiments that tested or extended the matching law, and because there were so many experiments running at the same time, there were always new data to discuss even though each experiment might take months to complete. Billy Baum and others have recently described the excitement of those years at Harvard, and it was a privilege to be part of the scene.[2]

Although the matching law has proven to have substantial generality in a variety of laboratory settings,

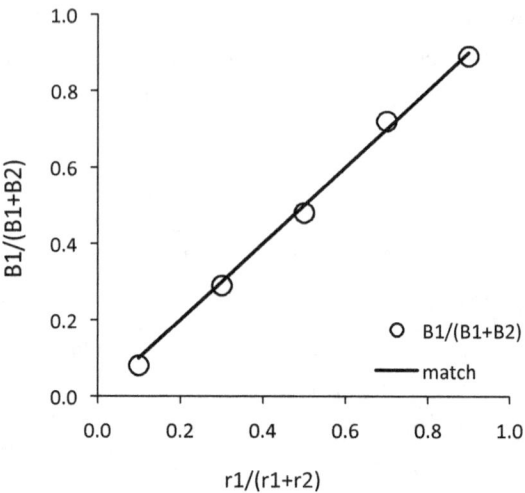

Figure 3.1. Hypothetical data illustrating the matching relation, Equation 3.1, between proportions of responses to two alternatives and proportions of reinforcers obtained from those alternatives.

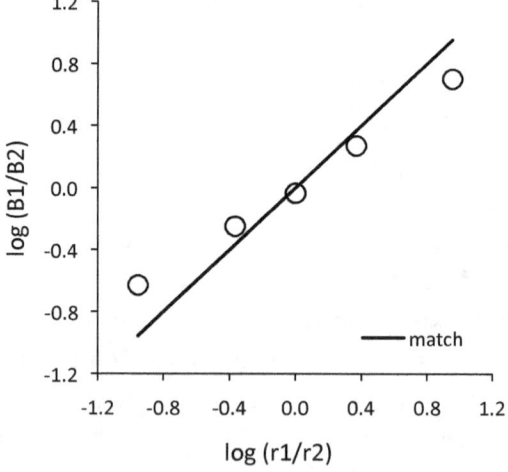

Figure 3.2. Hypothetical data illustrating undermatching between the logarithm of the ratio of responses to two alternatives and the logarithm of the ratio of reinforcers obtained from those alternatives. The solid line represents strict matching; see text for details

deviations known as undermatching and bias have often appeared in experimental data. To capture these deviations, Equation 3.1 may be restated as a power function relating behavior ratios and reinforcer ratios termed generalized matching:

$$\frac{B_1}{B_2} = c\left(\frac{r_1}{r_2}\right)^a .$$

(3.2)

In Equation 3.2, a represents the sensitivity of behavior ratios to reinforcer ratios, and c represents a bias toward B_1 or B_2 when the reinforcer ratio is 1.0. Equation 3.2 reduces to strict matching of response and reinforcer ratios when both a and c are 1.0.

Taking logarithms, Equation 3.2 becomes

$$\log\left(\frac{B_1}{B_2}\right) = a\log\left(\frac{r_1}{r_2}\right) + \log c .$$

(3.3)

(Readers can confirm this logarithmic transformation by referring back to Chapter 2.) Equation 3.3 is a linear function with slope a and intercept $\log c$. When response ratios are less extreme than reinforcer ratios – known as undermatching – a is less than 1.0, and when responding is biased – for example, a preference for the left key over the right key when the reinforcer ratio is 1.0 – the value of $\log c$ differs from 0, signifying that c does not equal 1.0. Equation 3.3 is illustrated with hypothetical data in Figure 3.2; the slope of a line fitted to these data points (not shown) is 0.7, clearly shallower than the strict matching line.

Both strict and generalized matching equations have been used to describe behavior in a remarkable variety of settings. In one of my favorite studies, Rand Conger, a sociologist, and Peter Killeen, who studied with Herrnstein at Harvard, invited individual college students to talk with three others, who were in fact confederates. One engaged the subject student in general conversation, and the other two (call them R1 and R2) made positive comments such as "Good point" at different variable intervals, signaled covertly by the experimenter, after the subject had addressed a remark to one of them. The proportion of time the subject spent addressing R1 or R2 roughly matched the proportion of positive comments made by R1 or R2, who were in effect acting like two keys for a pigeon with automatically programmed food reinforcers.[3]

Matching and response rate

From the strict matching law (Equation 3.1), Herrnstein derived a mathematical expression describing the relation between the rate of a single response and the rate of reinforcement obtained by that response.[4] The derivation assumes that the response being measured – key pecking, bar pressing, or the like – occurs in a context of other behavior that isn't specified or measured, and that this unspecified "other" behavior, designated B_o, has reinforcing consequences designated r_o. For example, r_o might be relief from discomfort that follows from scratching at an itch (B_o), or the entertainment value (r_o) of looking around the experimental chamber (B_o). Substituting B_o for B_2, Equation 3.1 becomes

$$\frac{B_1}{B_1 + B_O} = \frac{r_1}{r_1 + r_O}.$$

(3.4)

On the assumption that everything a creature does adds up to a constant k – implying that a creature is always doing something and that it can shift from one activity to another, but not increase or decrease its total activity – we can replace the denominator on the left with k and rearrange to obtain a hyperbolic function (see Chapter 2):

$$B_1 = \frac{kr_1}{r_1 + r_O}.$$

(3.5)

Here, k represents the asymptotic (maximum) response rate of B_1 as reinforcer rate r_1 goes toward infinity, and r_O represents rate of reinforcement for unmeasured alternative activities, expressed in units of food reinforcement. In words, Equation 3.5 states that the rate of a specified response depends on the rate of reinforcement obtained by that response relative to the total reinforcement obtained in the situation.

Equation 3.5, which is known as the "relative law of effect," or more descriptively as "Herrnstein's hyperbola," does an excellent job of describing the relation between response rate and reinforcer rate in a standard experiment where a variable-interval (VI) schedule is in effect for a number of consecutive experimental sessions, each lasting (say) an hour and conducted daily until response rate became stable – i.e., consistent from day to day (see Chapter 2). To evaluate the effect of the average interval between reinforcers (the inverse of the reinforcer rate),

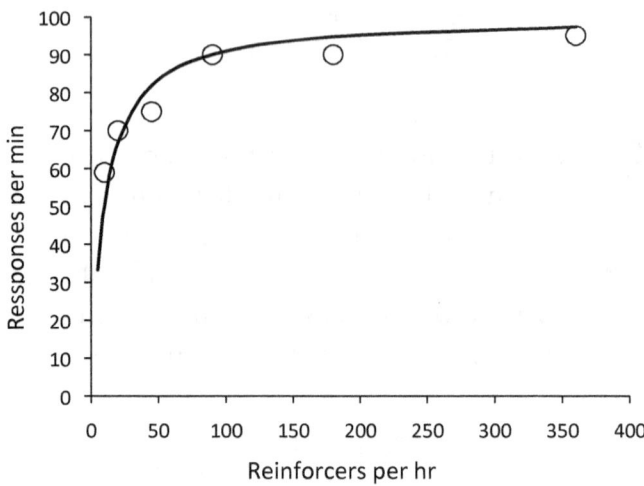

Figure 3.3. Hypothetical data showing steady-state response rate on VI schedules over the range from 6 minutes to 10 seconds, yielding between 10 to 360 reinforcers/hr. The solid line represents Herrnstein's hyperbola (Equation 3.5) with k = 100 and ro = 10.

the experimenter would then switch to another VI value, determine the stable response rate, switch to yet another VI value, and so on a series of successive conditions until enough different response rates maintained by different reinforcer rates had been studied to trace out a functional relation between them. Figure 3.3 illustrates Equation 3.5, with k = 100 and r_o = 10; the data are hypothetical. There is some debate, in the basic research literature, on the most appropriate mathematical form of the function and the interpretation of its parameters; here, we will consider its application to problem behavior.

Jack McDowell has applied Equation 3.5 to naturally occurring problem behavior: self-injurious scratching by a 10-year-old boy.[5] First, McDowell determined that the boy scratched most frequently while watching TV, and that scratching was apparently reinforced by verbal reprimands from family members. He recorded the number of times the boy scratched himself in a period of TV watching and the number of reprimands by family members in that same period, and showed that Equation 3.5 provided an excellent description of the relation between scratching rates and reprimand rates. He also noted that a method for reducing problem behavior follows from Equation 3.5: If the value of r_o is increased, scratching should decrease. The increase in r_o could be achieved by reinforcing some behavior other than scratching, or simply by providing reinforcers independently of responding. There are many examples of interventions of these sorts; we will consider them in later chapters.

Multiple schedules

As we have seen, Herrnstein's relative law of effect follows from the strict matching law for choice between two alternatives that are reinforced at different rates and are available at the same time – i.e., concurrent schedules. Before visiting Harvard, I had tinkered with a related procedure that arranges two different rates of reinforcement in a so-called *multiple* schedule, where each reinforcer rate is available for a fixed period and is signaled by a distinctive stimulus. Multiple schedules are like concurrent schedules in that two different reinforcer rates can be arranged for an individual subject within a single experimental session. But there's a big difference: In concurrent schedules the subject is free to switch between schedules at any time, whereas in multiple schedules, the experimenter controls the time during which the subject is stuck with each schedule. As a result, the experimenter can compare performances maintained by controlled

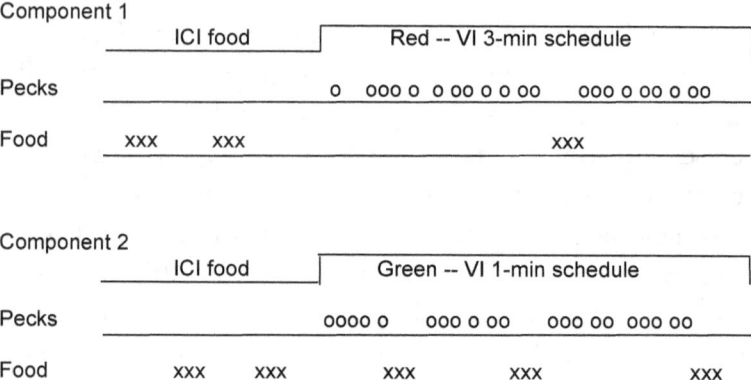

Figure 3.4. A multiple schedule with alternating components of fixed duration separated by intercomponent intervals (ICI). In one component, signaled by a red key light, food (xxx) follows a key peck (o) every 3 minutes on average (VI 3-min or 20 reinforcers/hr). In the other component, signaled by a green key light, food follows a peck every minute on average (VI 1-min or 60 reinforcers/hr). Food may also be presented at variable times (VT) during the ICI to disrupt responding..

exposure to different schedules within a single session, rather than between successive conditions that may be separated by weeks or months. In the experiment described at the beginning of Chapter 1, Shahan and Burke arranged a multiple schedule which permitted them to compare their two conditions – alcohol reinforcers only, or alcohol reinforcers plus free food – in this way. I had adopted the multiple schedule paradigm largely for this reason. As will be seen, the paradigm proved to be very important as research on behavioral momentum proceeded over the next three decades.

A time-line diagram of events in a multiple schedule is shown in Figure 3.4. Each stimulus and its associated schedule define a component of the multiple schedule.

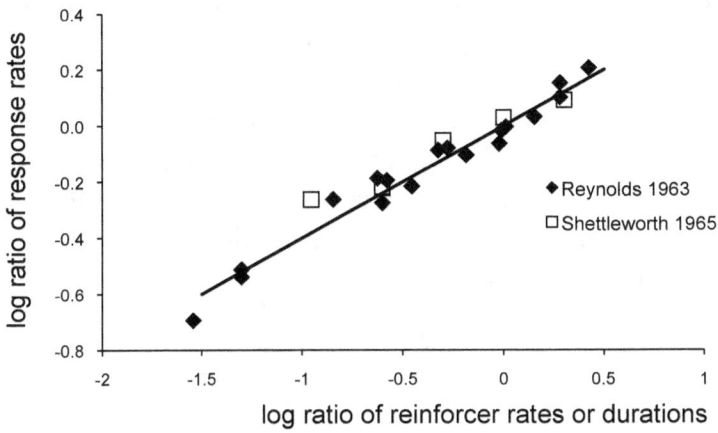

Figure 3.5. Data from Reynolds (1963, filled diamonds) and from Shettle-worth and Nevin (1965, open squares) relating the log ratios of response rates in two multiple-schedule components to the log ratio of reinforcer rates (Reynolds) or durations (Shettleworth). The solid line represents Equation 3.3 with $a = 0.4$, log $c = 0$.

George Reynolds, working at Harvard in 1963, obtained some strikingly orderly data with pigeons as subjects when he varied the reinforcer rates arranged by VI schedules independently in each of two components, and Sara Shettleworth, working in my lab at Swarthmore in 1964, obtained similar data with pigeons when she varied the durations (as opposed to rates) of food reinforcers in two components with the same VI schedule.[6] Figure 3.5 presents the average data from both studies expressed as the log ratios of response rates in the components, plotted against the log ratios of reinforcer rates or durations. The dashed line represents Equation 3.3 with $a = 0.4$ and log $c = 0.0$. Although the slope of the data for reinforcer duration (open squares) is a bit shallower than that for reinforcer rate, the agreement is close enough to suggest that reinforcer rate and duration are about equally effective as determiners of response rates in multiple schedules.

In order to bring his formulation of the relative law of effect (Equation 3.5) to bear on multiple schedules, Herrnstein suggested that response rates in one component were influenced by reinforcers in the other component, effectively contributing to the total reinforcement in the situation. Thus,

For Component 1,
$$B_1 = \frac{kr_1}{r_1 + mr_2 + r_o}$$
(3.6a)

and for Component 2,
$$B_2 = \frac{kr_2}{r_2 + mr_1 + r_o}$$
(3.6b)

where B_1 and B_2 are response rates and r_1 and r_2 are reinforcer rates in Components 1 and 2, and r_o, as above, is the food-reinforcer equivalent of how good it feels to engage in unmeasured activity. The parameter m scales the effectiveness of Component 2 reinforcers on responding in Component 1 and vice versa (m would presumably be about zero if the components were long and separated by several minutes, and might approach 1.0 if the components were short and alternated rapidly with no interval between them).

A number of experiments have evaluated Equations 3.6a and 3.6b by varying the reinforcer rates, r_1 and r_2, over a series of experimental conditions. It occurred to me that another approach was to keep r_1 and r_2 constant and to vary the denominators of both equations by adding explicit reinforcers in a third component. So upon returning to Swarthmore College after my year at Harvard, I set up a two-component multiple schedule with dark-key periods separating the components, as shown in Figure 3.4. In effect, the dark-key intercomponent interval (ICI) was a third component, and I could simply present food during the ICI at variable times regardless of whatever the pigeon was doing (a so-called VT schedule). Moreover, I could vary the rate of ICI food by varying the average time between food presentations across successive conditions.

Let's expand Equations 3.6a and 3.6b for multiple schedules to include ICI food, as in Herrnstein's own development:

For Component 1,
$$B_1 = \frac{kr_1}{r_1 + mr_2 + nr_{ICI} + r_O} \qquad (3.7a)$$

and for Component 2,
$$B_2 = \frac{kr_2}{r_2 + mr_1 + nr_{ICI} + r_O} . \qquad (3.7b)$$

All notation is as above, except that r_{ICI} represents the rate of ICI food and n scales its impact on the adjacent components.

The experiment ran as follows. Pigeons were trained to peck a key that was alternately lighted red or green. If it was green, food was available on a VI 1-minute schedule (transformed and abbreviated 60/hr), and if it was red, food was available on a VI 3-minute schedule (20/hr). Red-key and green-key components lasted for a minute each, and were presented in an irregular order separated by 30 second ICIs with the key darkened. The birds had previously been trained on various multiple schedules with white keys and superimposed black lines, so they pecked the red and green keys readily and response rates

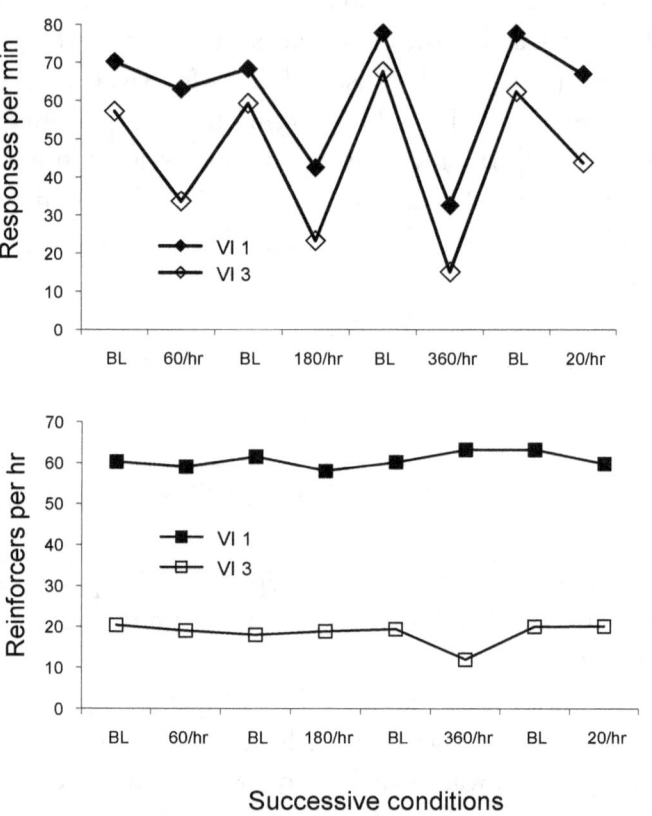

Figure 3.6. Upper panel: Average responses per minute in successive base-line determinations and in the first hour with ICI food in the VI 1-minute and VI 3-minute components of a multiple schedule. Lower panel: Obtained reinforcer rates in those components (from Nevin, 1974).

stabilized on the VI 1-minute and VI 3-minute schedules after 20-30 daily sessions lasting about 1 hour, defining the initial baseline response rates. I then introduced 60 food presentations per hour into the dark-key ICI and found – to my astonishment – that response rates in both components decreased abruptly, within a few minutes' exposure to the altered procedure, and then changed rather little over the next 9 sessions, after which I discontinued ICI food for 10 sessions to recapture baseline response rates. This cycle of baseline, ICI food, and baseline recovery was repeated several times, with 180, 360, and 20 ICI food presentations per hour, in that order, for 6-10 sessions. Figure 3.6 displays the results graphically. The upper panel shows that baseline response rates were always higher in the VI 1-minute component and that ICI food reduced response rates in both components; the reduction was generally greater in the VI 3-minute component. The lower panel shows that there was relatively little change in obtained reinforcer rates.

I sent a summary of the results to Richard Herrnstein and he included them in his 1970 article setting forth his formulation of the law of effect. Figure 3.7 shows that the data are very well described by Equations 3.7a and 3.7b with values of k, m, n, and r_0 given in the figure.

By the time I got around to publishing the full data set in 1974, I had started thinking about the situation in a new way. The idea was to treat ICI food differently from baseline reinforcement conditions, which never changed and were in effect continuously throughout the experiment. This made sense because ICI food had surprisingly abrupt disruptive effects – indeed, its effects were evident within a single session and changed rather little over additional

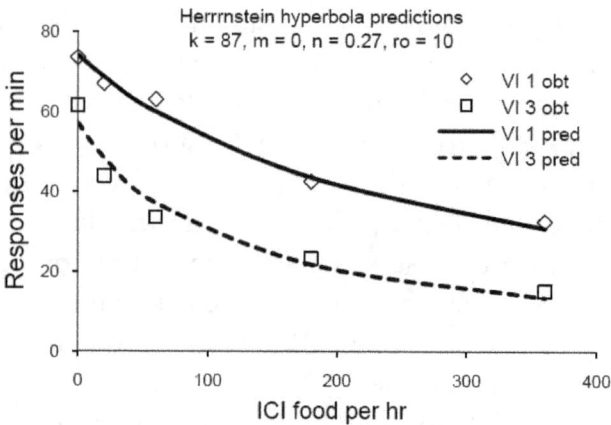

Figure 3.7. Data from Figure 3.6 plotted as functions of ICI food presentations per hour, together with the predictions of Equations 3.6a and 3.6b.

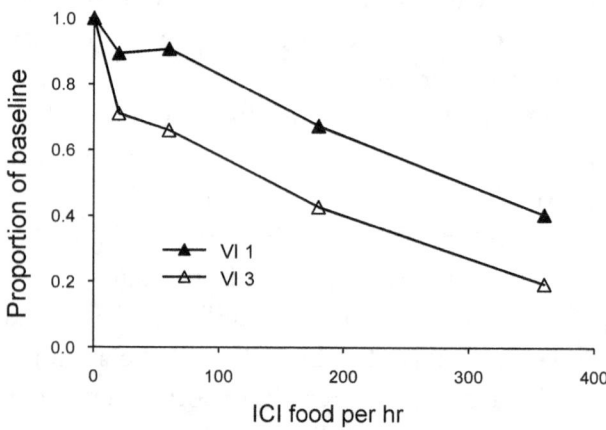

Figure 3.8. Data from Figure 3.6 replotted as proportions of response rates in the immediately preceding baseline determinations, as functions of ICI food presentations per hour (adapted from Nevin, 1974).

Table 3.1. Average rates of key pecking (resp/min) and obtained reinforcer rates (rft/hr) in the VI 1-minute (green) and VI 3-minute (red)
components of a multiple schedule during baseline (BL) and the first hour
of four ICI food disruptor tests. In the right columns, each response rate
with ICI food is expressed as the average proportion of the preceding
baseline. From Nevin (1974), Experiment 1.

ICI food	Resp/min		Rft/hr		Prop BL	
	VI 1	VI 3	VI 1	VI 3	VI 1	VI 3
0	70.2	57.2	60.3	20.3		
60/hr	73.1	33.6	59.0	19.0	0.91	0.66
0	68.3	590.3	61.5	18.0		
180	42.5	23.3	58.0	18.8	0.67	0.43
0	77.9	67.7	60.2	19.4		
360	32,5	15.2	63.2	12.0	0.41	0.19
0	77.7	62.4	63.2	20.0		
20	67.0	43.9	59.8	201.	0.89	0.71

sessions, unlike the usual month or so of daily sessions to
establish stable response rates in research on the steady-
state effects of reinforcement. With interest centering on
the strength of responding in the two components that
resulted from extended training on baseline conditions
of reinforcement, I suggested that "when some variable
that reduces response rates is introduced uniformly with
respect to both components, the component performance
that undergoes the smaller reduction, relative to baseline,
may be identified as the stronger of the two performances"
because it was more resistant to change.[7]

Figure 3.8 presents resistance functions relating
changes in responding to the rate of ICI food. It shows
that response rate, expressed as a proportion of the

immediately preceding baseline, decreased systematically with the rate of ICI food and was always greater in the VI 1-minute component. Thus, responding was more resistant to change in the component with more frequent reinforcement. The average data are presented in Table 3.1, so readers can confirm the data treatments described here.

Table 3.1 also permits calculation of a weighted mean proportion of baseline that was used as a summary measure of resistance to change in several subsequent studies. The measure, designated p_w, is calculated as $p_w = \Sigma(p_i {}^* x_i)/\Sigma x_i$, where p_i is the proportion of baseline obtained with the ith value of the disruptor, x_i. Thus, for the average data for the VI 1-minute component of Experiment 1,

$$p_w = \frac{0.89 {}^* 20 + 0.91 {}^* 60 + 0.67 {}^* 180 + 0.41 {}^* 360}{20 + 60 + 180 + 360} = 0.55.$$

The reader may wish to confirm that p_w for the VI 3-minute component is 0.32. Although p_w is useful for summarizing ordinal differences between components within an experiment, it should be used with caution because it does not have the properties of an interval or ratio scale, precluding meaningful addition, subtraction, multiplication, or division. For example, one should not say that responding in the VI 1-minute component was $0.55/0.32 = 1.72$ times more resistant to ICI food than in the VI 3-minute component.

A second experiment, conducted earlier at Swarthmore with Sara Shettleworth, used another standard method for reducing response rate: Withholding food altogether, a widely studied process called extinction (see Chapter 7).

The data showed that resistance to extinction after training on VI schedules, like resistance to ICI food, was greater in the component with more frequent reinforcement. Two further experiments with equal VI schedules showed that resistance to ICI food was greater in a component with larger or less delayed reinforcers. (Sara also had reported greater resistance to extinction in a component with longer-duration reinforcers.[6]) All in all, these four experiments showed that response rate was more resistant to change in the richer component – i.e., with more frequent, larger, or less delayed reinforcers. A fifth experiment will be discussed in Chapter 6.

In 1974 I suggested that resistance to change was a good general measure of the strength of responding. As noted in Chapter 1, Kendon Smith published a theoretical article in the same year, arguing that a good measure of the strength of responding was the magnitude of some opposed variable that would exactly cancel the effect of reinforcement. In effect, this is an extreme version of resistance to change; for example, in my data in Figure 3.8, Smith's suggestion is equivalent to finding the rates of ICI food that would bring response rates all the way down to 0. The main point is that Smith's article added some general theoretical support to my identification of "strength" with resistance to change.

A review of multiple-schedule studies by other researchers that could be interpreted in terms of resistance to change showed that this result was quite general. For example, response rate in the richer of two components was more resistant to disruption by response-contingent electric shocks, by signals that preceded unavoidable electric shocks, by abrupt changes in food deprivation, and by

Table 3.2. Summary of results of multiple-schedule studies comparing resistance to change in rich and lean components.

Difference in conditions of reinforcement between components

Disruptor	Rft rate	Rft amt	Rft delay	Rft prob
ICI food	+	+	+	
Extinction	+	+	+	--
Punishment	+			
Deprivation	+			
Signaled shock	+	+		
Response effort		+		+

abrupt increases in the number of responses required to obtain reinforcers. In 1979, I assembled the results of all the relevant published studies into a table like Table 3.2, where + indicates greater resistance to change in the richer, more favorable component and - indicates the reverse result.[8]

Obviously, there were lots of empty cells, and subsequent research has filled in many of them – nearly always repeating the general finding of greater resistance in the richer component. I also noted that resistance to change generally agreed with the results of experiments that allowed subjects to choose between conditions of reinforcement differing in rate, amount, delay, or probability of reinforcement: Not surprisingly, the richer alternative was usually preferred. An obvious point of disagreement arises in the cell for reinforcer probability and extinction, where subjects prefer the alternative with the higher probability (e.g., 1.0 or FR1) but usually exhibit greater resistance to extinction in the condition with the lower probability (e.g., 0.25 or VR 4). Because resistance to extinction is clinically important and has been studied so extensively, this discrepancy raised important questions that will be addressed at length in Chapter 7.

At the end of Chapter 2, I asserted that the pigeon data on resistance to change were difficult to distinguish from those of humans. It's time to back up that assertion; but first I acknowledge with pleasure that momentum research with humans got a big boost from Bud Mace. After he and his colleagues published a paper entitled "Behavioral momentum in the treatment of noncompliance" in 1988 (to be discussed in Chapter 9), we became friends, and he suggested a systematic replication of my pigeon work with adults with mental retardation living in a group home.

Bud and his students began with a variation of the basic multiple VI VI schedule paradigm discussed above. They asked two group-home residents to sort colored plastic utensils and gave them small amounts of popcorn or coffee on VI schedules for sorting correctly. Some of the dinnerware was green and some was red, and the residents were asked to sort one color for a while and then sort the other color (thus defining two multiple-schedule components). If they were sorting red dinnerware, they received popcorn or coffee according to a VI 60-s schedule (60/hr), and if they were sorting green dinnerware, they received popcorn or coffee on a VI 240-s schedule (15/hr). After several days, this routine had established stable baseline sorting rates in each component. Then, sorting was disrupted by turning on an adjacent TV set with a favorite MTV show. Although both subjects had similar baseline sorting rates in both components, sorting was more resistant to distraction by the MTV show in the

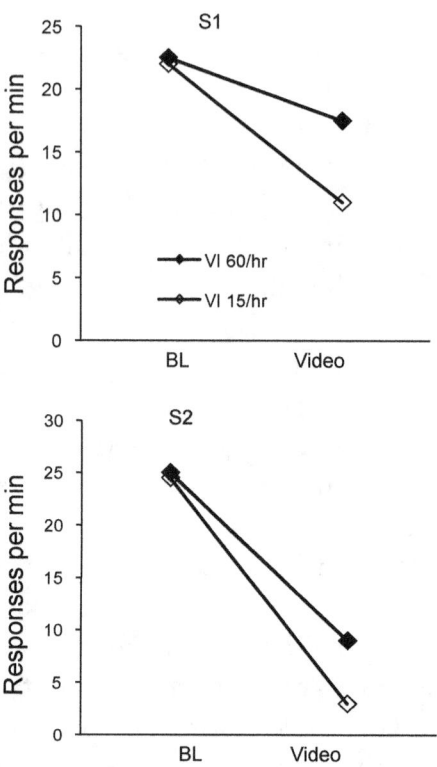

Figure 3.9 Rates of sorting utensils for two group-home residents in multiple VI VI schedules. Baseline sorting rates (BL) were disrupted by playing an MTV program. Adapted from Mace et al. (1990).

richer VI 60-s component, pretty much like the pigeon data in Figure 3.7. Mace's individual data appear in Figure 3.9 (See also Chapter 5).[9]

A related experiment was conducted in 1996 by Steven Cohen at Bloomsburg State University with university students as subjects, using points that could be exchanged for credit in a psychology course as reinforcers for correctly typing words displayed on a computer monitor.

Multiple-schedule components were defined by the color on the monitor screen. In one study, Cohen arranged different reinforcer rates according to VI schedules (a second study will be described in Chapter 5). Typing was disrupted by providing a puzzle book ("Where's Waldo?") that distracted the students from the task. The results were at least ordinally similar to those obtained by Mace with group-home residents: Response rates were more resistant to distraction in the richer schedule component.[10]

A study with college students and older adults by Joseph Plaud and his associates has confirmed the similarity of human and pigeon data with reinforcers that differed in magnitude rather than rate.[11] Plaud's subjects pressed computer keys in multiple VI VI schedules with the same reinforcer rate, but where the reinforcer was 10 tokens in one component and 1 token in the other. Tokens could be exchanged for a chance to win $50 in a lottery. Under a variety of contingency changes including extinction, response rates were more resistant to change in the large-reinforcer component, as found with pigeons by Sara Shettleworth and in Experiment 3 of my 1974 study .

In the foregoing examples, the responses selected for study were more or less arbitrary and chosen for convenience, so there is not much practical value in increasing (or decreasing) their persistence. By contrast, the persistence of engagement in academic activities in special education classrooms for children with intellectual and developmental disabilities is essential for learning. Can persistence be enhanced by frequent reinforcement, despite ongoing problem behavior such as physical disruption or aggression, repetitive vocalizing, or self-stimulation?

To explore this question, Diana Parry-Cruwys and

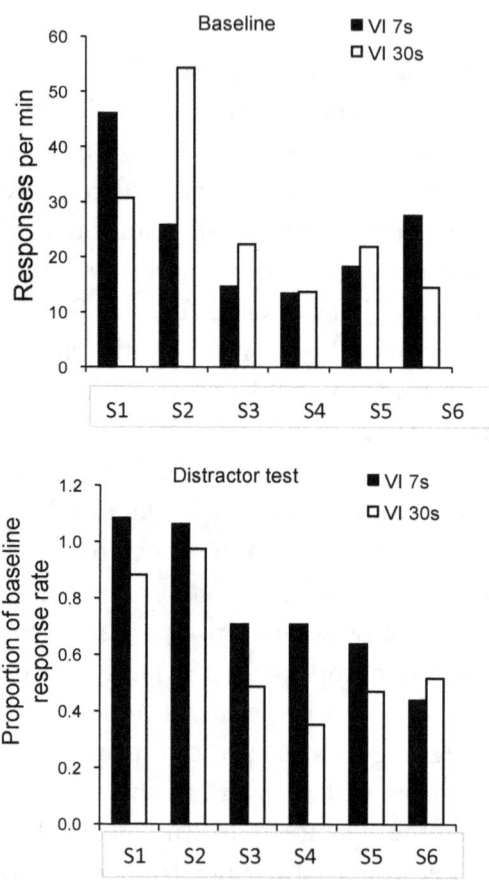

Figure 3.10. The upper panel presents the rates of engagement by children with developmental disabilities in classroom tasks with different rates of reinforcement on VI schedules. The lower panel shows the proportions of baseline during distraction. Adapted from Parry-Cruwys et al. (2012)

colleagues at the New England Center for Children and the Shriver Center studied six children with developmental disabilities in a special-education classroom. They arranged tokens or edible reinforcers for engagement in familiar activities (e.g., jigsaw puzzles, academic worksheets). For each participant, two different tasks alternated, with reinforcers given on a VI 7-s schedule for one task and on a VI 30-s schedule for the other. Thus, one task was correlated with a high rate of reinforcement and the other was correlated with a lower rate of reinforcement. Resistance to disruption was measured by presenting a distracting item (e.g., an interesting video). The upper panel of Figure 3.10 shows that across children, response rates were about equally likely to be higher or lower in the richer VI 7-s component. The lower panel displays proportions of baseline during distraction expressed relative to preceding baseline components. Persistence was greater in the richer VI 7-s component for five of six participants, and there is no obvious relation between differences in baseline response rate and proportions of baseline.[12]

In summary, it appears that the effects of reinforcement on resistance to change in pigeons can be replicated with normal and developmentally disabled humans, both children and adults, with a variety of responses and reinforcers, in a reasonably wide range of experimental and natural settings including the special-ed classroom. Importantly, there was no consistent evidence that resistance to change was related to rates of responding before disruption. Chapter 4 will suggest that response rates and resistance to change are independent aspects of behavior that can be related to each other through the metaphor of behavioral momentum.

Chapter 4

The Momentum Metaphor

According to Newton's first law of motion, a body remains at rest or continues to move in a straight line unless acted upon by an external force. According to his second law, any change of motion is directly proportional to the imposed force and inversely proportional to the mass of the body. The results of my 1974 Experiment 1, reviewed in Chapter 3, suggested that something analogous might be going on for behavior. If steady-state conditions were kept constant – including the presentation of reinforcers according to baseline contingencies of reinforcement – the rates of responding in the two alternating multiple-schedule components would continue unchanged, session after session. When free food was introduced during the interval between components, like an external force, response rate decreased, like a decrease in the velocity of a physical body. Moreover, the magnitude of the decrease depended directly on the ICI food rate and inversely on the steady-state rate of reinforcement in the schedule components. In addition, some of the data described in Chapter 3 suggested that response rates and resistance to change were independent of each other, as for the velocity and mass of a body in motion. As a former student of engineering, I found the parallels too suggestive to resist, and checked out a physics text to confirm my 30-year-old recollections.

Measuring behavioral mass

In physics, Newton's second law is stated as

$$\Delta v = f / m, \tag{4.1}$$

where Δv is the change in velocity and f is the imposed force. Translating into behavior,

$$\Delta B = -x / m \tag{4.2}$$

where ΔB is the change in response rate and x is the value of the disruptor, which gets a minus sign here because response rate decreases during disruption. Behavioral mass m has to be inferred from the change in response rate during disruption x, such as the introduction of ICI food in my 1974 study (Chapter 3).

In 1974, I had expressed the effects of a disruptor as the proportion of the preceding baseline response rate, as in Figure 3.8, but proportion of baseline has limitations. Consider a case where baseline response rate in two multiple-schedule components, C1 and C2, is 100 pecks per minute, and a disruptor reduces the rate to 60/min in C1 and to 30/min in C2, or 0.6 and 0.3 as proportions of baseline. The difference between them – 0.3 – is substantial relative to the full range from 1.0 to 0.0. But if a more potent disruptor had reduced them to 4/min in C1 and 2/min in C2, or 0.04 and 0.02 as proportions of baseline, the difference between them is small relative to the range from 1.0 to 0.0. We can still say that responding is more resistant to change in C1

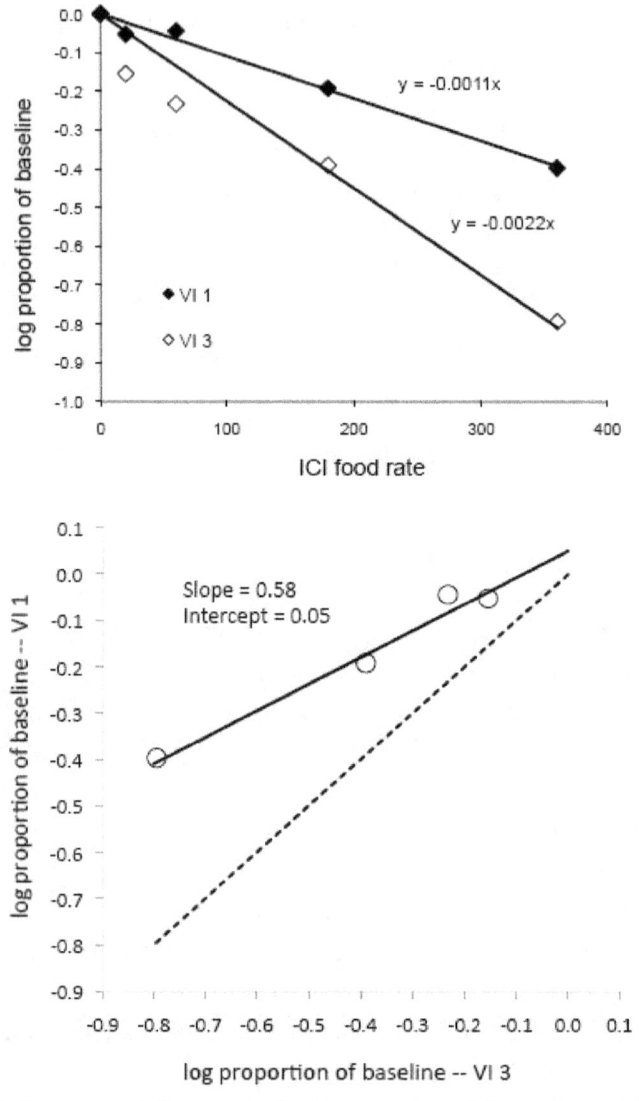

Fig. 4.1. Upper panel: Resistance functions replotted from Figure 3.8 as log proportions of baseline; slopes estimated by the method of least squares are indicated for each function. Lower panel: Log proportions of baseline in the VI 1 component plotted against corresponding log proportions of baseline in the VI 3 component; see text for explanation. Redrawn from data of Nevin (1974).

78

than C2, so that's ordinal agreement across disruptors. But a logarithmic transformation, which converts equal ratios into equal differences (see Chapter 2), permits a stronger statement: log(0.6) - log (0.3) = 0.30, and log(0.04) - log (0.02) = 0.30, so the difference in resistance to change, stated as log proportions of baseline, is the same for the moderate and potent disruptors. And that is as it should be: The difference in the strength of responding established by different histories of reinforcement should be invariant with respect to the potency of the disruptor.

If ΔB is expressed as the logarithm of the proportion of baseline, B_x/B_o, where B_x is response rate during disruption and B_o is baseline response rate, then by the rules of logarithms, $\log(B_x/B_o) = \log(B_x)-\log(B_o)$, so ΔB is simply the change in log response rates. Now let's rewrite Equation 4.2:

$$\log\left(\frac{Bx}{Bo}\right) = -\frac{x}{m}. \qquad (4.3)$$

Thus, if x is constant, the log proportion of baseline is directly proportional to the reciprocal of behavioral mass – that is, the greater the mass, the smaller the change in responding when disrupted by x. When x is varied (with m presumed constant), the right side of the equation is the slope of the resistance function – the average change in $\log(B_x/B_o)$ per unit change in x over the entire range of x-values – so an experiment that varies the potency of a disruptor across conditions with the same reinforcer rate can give an estimate of behavioral mass.

The upper panel of Figure 4.1 shows that resistance functions for VI 1-min (60 reinforcers/hr) and VI 3-min (20

reinforcers/hr) when ICI food rate was varied from 20/hr
to 360/hr (See Chapter 3) are tolerably linear in this form.
Their slopes, calculated by the method of least squares (or
estimated by your computer) are -0.0011 and -.0022. Because
behavioral mass is inversely related to the slope (Equation
4.3), the conclusion is that behavioral mass in the VI
1-minute component, m_1, was twice that in the VI 3-minute
component, m_2.

However, the x-axis scale is arbitrary: ICI food rate
could have been stated as reinforcers per min or per sec, so
we cannot assign an absolute value to m_1 or m_2 – only their
ratio can be estimated. (A similar problem arises in ordinary
measures of weight, which could be ounces or grams. That
problem is resolved by international agreement to refer all
weights to a standard kilogram, which is a cast-iron hexagon
equal in weight to 1000 cc of water. No such standard exists
for operant behavior.)

There is a more direct way to get at the mass ratio. If we
plot $\log(B_{x1}/B_{o1})$ against $\log(B_{x2}/B_{o2})$ at each value of x, where
subscripts 1 and 2 represent the VI 1-min and VI 3-min
components, respectively, we get a graph of the relation

$$\log\left(\frac{B_{x1}}{B_{o1}}\right) = [m_2/m_1]\log\left(\frac{B_{x2}}{B_{o2}}\right) \qquad (4.4)$$

where the slope of the function is the inverse ratio of the
two behavioral masses. This approach assumes that the
effective value of x is the same for both components, but
does not care what that value is because $-x$ disappears from
the analysis. To get a quantitative estimate of m_2/m_1, we
have to fit a so-called structural relation; the rationale and

80

calculation are explained in Davison and McCarthy's book on the matching law[1].

The lower panel of Figure 4.1 presents the data in the form suggested by Equation 4.4; the solid line is the best fitting structural relation, with its slope and intercept shown in the figure. Because there is a non-zero intercept, Equation 4.4 cannot be exactly correct, and we will not use this approach to evaluating mass ratios again. Note, however, that this way of plotting data reveals at once which of the two components exhibits ordinally greater resistance to change: If the data points are above the diagonal dashed line, representing equality of $\log(B_{x1}/B_{o1})$ and $\log(B_{x2}/B_{o2})$, responding is more resistant to change in Component 1 than in Component 2, and vice versa. The data need not conform to a linear relation – indeed, they can be quite irregular – and the value of the disruptor need not be quantified, unlike the slope calculation in the upper panel of Figure 4.1.

At UNH in 1983, Charlotte Mandell, Jean (Roberts) Atak, and I replicated my 1974 Experiment 1 with six pigeons, three different reinforcer rates, and with extinction as well as ICI food as disruptors.[2] The data were pretty orderly, so we attempted to quantify the effects of reinforcer rate on behavioral mass. Our published approach to extracting a term representing behavioral mass proved to be cumbersome and required visual judgment; it has never (to my knowledge) been used subsequently. So here I pass up the opportunity to review it and instead fit slopes of resistance functions in the same way as for the 1974 data in Figure 4.1. Figure 4.2 presents the data for the effects of ICI food on log proportions of baseline for the three pairs of VI schedules together with straight lines fitted in the same way as in Figure 4.1. The fits are tolerable for the richer

81

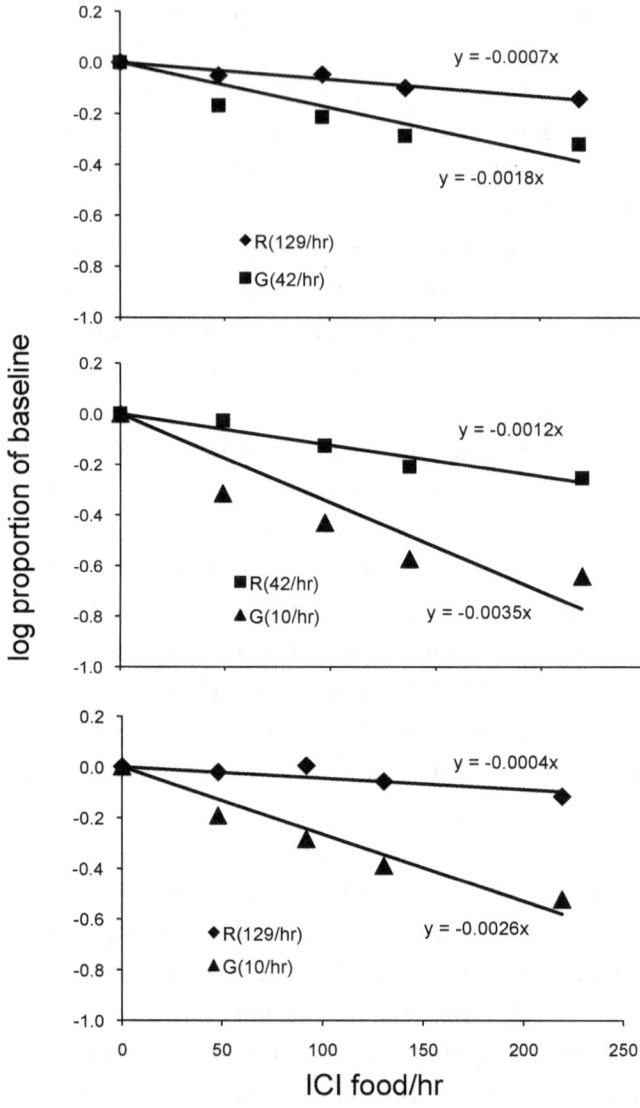

Figure 4.2. Resistance functions relating log proportions of baseline response rate to intercomponent food rate for three pairs of multiple schedules with key colors and reinforcer rates indicated. Slopes estimated by the method of least squares are indicated for each function. Redrawn from data of Nevin et al. (1983).

component in each pair, but the data depart from linearity in the leaner component. Nevertheless, the slopes are reasonably representative of the differences between components and pairs of schedules, and are given for each resistance function in Figure 4.2.

With ICI food as the disruptor, the slope ratios stand, approximately, in a simple relation to each other that corresponds to the requirements of physical measurement. In classical physics, where mass is measured on a ratio scale, the mass ratio for object A relative to object C necessarily equals the product of mass ratios A/B and B/C.

When Charlotte and Jean and I did our visual estimates of mass ratios, we got 2.5 for 129/hr *vs* 42/hr, 3.3 for 42/hr *vs* 10/hr, and 8.3 for 129/hr *vs* 10/hr. The product of 2.5 and 3.3 is 8.25, essentially the same as 8.3, the independently estimated mass ratio for 129/hr *vs* 10/hr, confirming ratio-scale measurement of behavioral mass. Pretty cool. But did our subjective evaluations somehow bias our ratio estimates to produce equality?

It turns out that the ratios of behavioral masses estimated from inverse ratios of resistance-function slopes, which are totally objective given the data, come close to behaving similarly. As shown in Table 4.1, mass ratios increase as reinforcer ratios increase. Moreover, for a reinforcer ratio of 129 *vs* 10 reinforcers/hour, the inverse slope ratio m_{129}/m_{10} is 6.5; the inverse slope ratio for m_{129}/m_{42} is 2.6; and the inverse slope ratio for m_{42}/m_{10} is 2.9. If the mass ratio m_{129}/m_{10} was exactly equal to the product of mass ratios m_{129}/m_{42} and m_{42}/m_{10}, it would be 7.6, the product of 2.6 and 2.9, which is not wildly different from the obtained value of 6.5. If the slope of the 10/hr resistance function in the bottom panel had been estimated at 0.0030 rather

Table 4.1. Baseline response rates and the ratio of behavioral masses in three two-component multiple VI VI schedules estimated by fitting straight lines to resistance functions (Figure 4.2), with baseline reinforcer rates and ratios indicated. Recalculated from data of Nevin et al. (1983).

Baseline B/min C1 C2	Baseline rft/hr C1 C2	Rft rate ratio (C1/C2)	Inverse ratio of slopes $1/(m_1/m_2)$ ICI food	Ext
83.9 89.5	129 42	3.1	2.6	1.6
94.7 68.5	42 10	4.2	2.9	1.5
93.5 50.7	129 10	12.9	6.5	1.4

than 0.0026, the agreement would have been exact – and inspection of the data suggests that a steeper slope might have been more representative of the first three data points.

With extinction as the disruptor, matters are less satisfactory. Table 4.1 shows that for the 1983 data, the slope ratios are greater than 1.0 in every case, indicating that responding in the richer component is more resistant to extinction than in the leaner component – in ordinal agreement with expectation – but they do not increase with the reinforcer ratio. I will argue in Chapter 7 that extinction requires special treatment to achieve quantitative agreement with other estimates of behavioral mass and to understand ordinal disagreements exemplified by the well-known partial-reinforcement extinction effect (PREE).

Years later, I realized that the entire enterprise was misguided because it assumed, for example, the behavioral mass of a discriminated operant maintained by 42 reinforcers/hr had a fixed value, regardless of whether the alternated schedule was richer (129/hr) or leaner (10/hr).

Chapter 5 describes a study undertaken for rather different reasons that found an inverse relation between resistance to change in a constant reinforcer-rate component and the reinforcer rate in alternated component. Thus, the value of behavioral mass in a component depends on the overall context of reinforcement; and examining Figure 4.2 from this perspective, the same sort of dependence is evident in the slopes for the 42/hr components. The slope of the resistance function for the 42/hr component is -0.0012 when the alternated component was 10/hr, and -0.0018 when the alternated component was 129/hr. In more general terms, the resistance to change of responding maintained by a multiple-schedule component with a constant reinforcer rate was inversely related to the reinforcer rate in an alternated component.

Looking back at the raw data, some 30 years after the fact, I found that all six pigeons exhibited this difference in slopes. Well, I missed it at the time, probably because of my pursuit of conformity to Newtonian physics. I am glad to set matters straight here, and to provide a lesson to readers: Let your analyses be guided by the data rather than your expectations (or hopes). However, my lapse should not detract from the orderliness of the relation between resistance to change and reinforcer rates, nor from the agreement with preference for different schedules of reinforcement described below.

Resistance to change, behavioral mass, and preference

In the momentum metaphor, the mass-like term is inferred from resistance to change and is closely akin to inertial mass. Physicists measure inertial mass by the rate of change of velocity (acceleration – see Eq. 4.1). A simple conceptual model proposed by Ernst Mach, a 19th-century physicist, for measuring inertial mass relative to a standard is to place two lumps into ideal, weightless, frictionless carts with a spring between them. The lump in Cart A is designated as a standard mass – say, 1 kg. Now, press the carts together and release abruptly so the spring sends them in opposite directions. If Cart B accelerates twice as fast as Cart A, as measured by the increase in velocity from zero in a brief period, its inertial mass must be half of that in Cart A, so the lump in Cart B is assigned a mass of 0.5 kg.

Physicists can also measure mass via Newton's law of gravitation, which states that the force of attraction between two bodies is given by the product of their gravitational masses divided by the square of the distance between them (the "inverse square" law). The conceptual model involves three lumps, A, B, and C, where A is designated the standard 1-kg lump as in the cart model for measuring inertial mass. Hang A and C from infinitely long weightless strings so that they are separated by distance d, and measure the force of attraction between them; call it f_{AC}. Then do the same with B and C and measure f_{BC}. Then, by the law of gravitation,

$$f_{AC} = (m_{A^*}m_C)/d^2$$
$$\text{and } f_{BC} = (m_{B^*}m_C)/d^2$$

Dividing these expressions and simplifying,

$$f_{AC}/f_{BC} = m_A/m_B. \tag{4.5}$$

Therefore, if $f_{AC} = 2f_{BC}$, $m_A = 2m_B$, so $m_B = 0.5$ kg. Note that we do not need to know the mass of lump C to reach this conclusion.

In principle, the gravitational mass of lump B relative to the standard lump A need not be the same as its inertial mass, but in physics they are the same for reasons that Einstein made clear in his theory of special relativity. Might a similar equality hold for inertial and gravitational versions of behavioral mass? To explore the question, Randy Grace and I conducted a series of experiments that measured both the relative resistance to change established by different rates of reinforcement and the degree of preference between those reinforcer rates, where preference was construed as the metaphorical equivalent of the relative force of attraction. The first of our efforts was described in our general review article entitled "Behavioral Momentum and the Law of Effect," published in *Behavioral and Brain Sciences* with commentary in 2000.[3]

Our original procedure included a conventional two-component multiple schedule and, in a separate part of the same session, a concurrent-chains procedure with the multiple-schedule components as their terminal links. Because we haven't considered concurrent chains before, some explanation is needed. A standard procedure is diagrammed in Figure 4.3. In the initial links, two keys are lighted white, and pecking either key produces its terminal link according to the same VI schedule. For example, pecking the left key could produce a change from white to red light, signaling the left terminal link, after an average of 30 seconds. Likewise, pecking the right key could produce a change from white to green, signaling the right terminal link, also after an average of 30 seconds. When either key changes color, the other key goes dark. Thus, the initial links were available at the same time, as in concurrent schedules of food reinforcement (see Chapter 3), and the proportion of choices to one or the

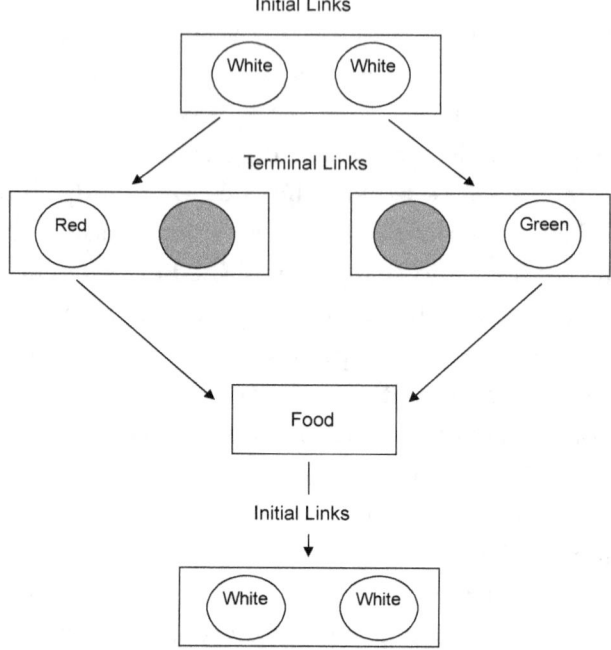

Fig. 4.3. A diagram of the concurrent-chains procedure used to estimate preference between terminal links signaled by red and green key lights.

other key during the initial links would indicate the pigeon's preference for one or the other terminal link. By contrast, the terminal links were available successively, as in multiple schedules.

Since Autor introduced this procedure in 1960 in his doctoral dissertation art Harvard, many experiments have arranged terminal links with variable-interval (VI) schedules of food reinforcement that ended when food was presented. A typical experiment varied the average time to food in each of the terminal links and measured the proportion or the ratio of initial-link pecks that produced the terminal links.

The well-nigh universal result is that the ratio of initial-link pecks to the left key was an increasing function of the ratio of reinforcer rates – the reciprocals of the VI schedules – in the terminal links. A number of comprehensive models of concurrent-chains performance, among them the "Contextual choice model" or CCM, proposed by Randy Grace in his doctoral dissertation at UNH, were developed after Autor's initial study, all of which described this basic finding. Their details are not critical for research on behavioral momentum so I will not pursue them here.[4]

Because the terminal links of concurrent chains are presented successively, they are like the components of a multiple schedule – except, of course, that the pigeon can indicate which terminal link it prefers by the allocation of its initial-link responses. In terms of the Newtonian metaphor, initial-link choices could be construed as measuring the relative attractiveness (gravitational pull?) of the two terminal links. Accordingly, Randy and I asked how their relative attractiveness might be related to relative resistance to change (inertial mass) in multiple-schedule components that were identical to the terminal links but presented successively by the experimenter rather than produced by the pigeon's key pecks.

Between 1997 and 2002, Randy and I conducted 8 experiments (some of them in collaboration with Melissa Bedell, an undergraduate at UNH, and some with Ant McLean and Shasta Holland at the University of Canterbury), which evaluated preference in the initial links of concurrent chains and resistance to change in the multiple-schedule equivalent of the terminal links.[5] In most of our studies, concurrent chains were arranged in one half of a session and multiple schedules were arranged in the other half, separated by a time out. In that way, we could examine both preference and multiple-schedule performance within subjects and sessions. In most cases, we measured resistance to food presented during intervals between the multiple-schedule components (ICI) without the concurrent chains; in one study we measured resistance in the terminal links themselves by suspending the initial-link schedules and presenting noncontingent food, effectively treating the initial link as if it were an intercomponent interval. Experiments differed in whether terminal links and components ended with food reinforcers after a variable duration, or lasted for a fixed duration with standard VI schedules as in the studies discussed above; whether reinforcers were the same or different in magnitude; and whether the schedules were VI or VR. In every case, we used a variable-time VT 10-s (360/hr) schedule of ICI (or initial-link) noncontingent food as a disruptor and calculated the slopes: $\log(B_{x1}/B_{o1})/x$ and $\log(B_{x2}/B_{o2})/x$, where x is 360/hr. These numbers gave us $1/m_1$ and $1/m_2$ (see Equation 4.4).

We also recorded the initial-link response rates, and expressed preference as the log ratio of initial-link responses, $\log(B_{i1}/B_{i2})$, or equivalently, $\log(B_{i1}) - \log(B_{i2})$, which is analogous to the difference in attractiveness between m_1 and m_2 in the Newtonian metaphor. If $[\log(B_{x1}/B_{o1})/x] - [\log(B_{x2}/B_{o2})/x] = \log(B_{i1}) - \log(B_{i2})$, the implication is that the differences between the behavioral equivalents of inertial and gravitational mass were the same, as for physical objects.[6]

When we correlated the differential resistance to ICI food with preference during sessions just before the ICI food test, we got a spectacularly orderly result (but definitely not equality) as shown in Figure 4.4. It appears that, at least for the pigeon and food reinforcers, the difference

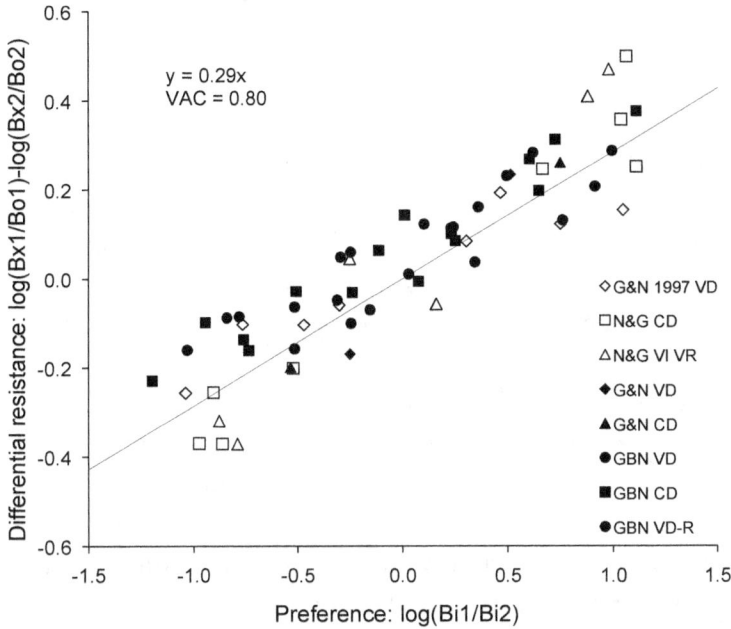

Figure 4.4. The relation between differential resistance to ICI food between two successively available schedule components, on the y-axis, and preference between those schedule components on the x axis, as determined in the initial links of concurrent chains; the legend indicates the published source. From Grace et al. (2002).

in the attractiveness of two schedule components and the difference in resistance to change in those components are linked by a simple linear function with slope 0.29. This is a structural relation showing how one dependent variable is related to another dependent variable without specifying the independent variables that gave rise to their values, such as VI *vs* VR or fixed- *vs* variable-duration terminal links. This convergence of independent measures of preference and resistance to change onto a single structural relation suggests a common underlying determiner of both measures that might be termed strength, value, or in metaphorical terms, behavioral mass.

Conclusion

This chapter began by invoking the metaphor of behavioral momentum, but I have not explicitly quantified the metaphor. In physics, momentum is given by the product of velocity and mass, mv, so by analogy, behavioral momentum would be given by mB, where B is the steady-state baseline rate of responding and m is behavioral mass, measured as the slope of a resistance function. In his comment on the *Behavioral and Brain Sciences* article that Randy and I published in 2000, Peter Killeen showed mathematically that behavioral momentum is the total of all behavior, measured in responses per unit time, under the resistance function as x goes to infinity – provided that the function is exponential with exponent $-x/m$. My 1974 data, shown as responses per minute in Figure 3.5, are pretty well described by exponential decreasing functions like that in Figure 2.3 – about as well as by Herrnstein's hyperbola – so I thank Peter for that elegant mathematical contribution (and for his friendship over many years).

But now, on behalf of readers who have slogged through this complicated exposition of the metaphor, we have to ask: Is it useful? Its quantitative particulars, such as the slope of the relation between resistance and preference, may be unique to pigeons, key pecking, VI schedules, food reinforcers, and ICI food disruptors; but the basic idea has found its way into a number of areas because it is intuitively easy to grasp. I often begin talks to nonspecialized audiences with an example. Imagine two superficially identical trucks (with invisible loads) traveling at the same speed along a highway under the same conditions of wind and road surface. Can you tell which one is more heavily loaded? Not until you do something like blocking the road with barricades. The audience gets it: The heavier truck smashes through the barricades with relatively little change in speed, whereas the lighter truck is slowed substantially. By analogy, you can't tell which of two ongoing responses occurring at the same rate – the traditional measure of response strength – has acquired a greater propensity to keep going as a result of its history of reinforcement until you challenge or disrupt responding in some way. Most importantly, the persistence of ongoing responding is separable from its rate. In a more qualitative vein, the next chapter will pursue the notion that ongoing response rate and resistance to change are determined independently by response-reinforcer and stimulus-reinforcer contingencies.

Chapter 5

Operant and Pavlovian Determiners of Resistance to Change

To review briefly: Chapter 3 concluded that response rate was more resistant to change in a multiple-schedule component with richer, more generous conditions of reinforcement, and that this difference in resistance to change was not related to differences in response rate between components before disruption. Chapter 4 concluded that the metaphor of behavioral momentum, together with relations between resistance to change and preference, could provide an avenue into the measurement of two related constructs in learning theory: Response strength and reinforcement value, represented in the metaphor as behavioral mass. Here, we will consider research that has tried to identify the processes that determine the strength of responding in a multiple-schedule component. Because the interest is in ordinal comparisons of resistance to change, we will employ the weighted average of the proportions of baseline (see p_{w} Chapter 3) rather than fitted slopes of resistance functions as the primary dependent variables.

94

Stimulus-reinforcer relations and resistance to change

There are two sorts of procedural relations or contingencies between a stimulus and the schedule it signals. First, the stimulus signals the availability of reinforcers according to an operant response-reinforcer contingency specified by the experimenter's procedure. Second, because reinforcers occur in the presence of the stimulus, it enters into a Pavlovian stimulus-reinforcer relation (see Chapter 1 for a discussion of response-reinforcer and stimulus-reinforcer contingencies embedded in a discriminated operant). Between 1984 and 2003, my colleagues and I conducted a number of experiments designed to separate the contributions of operant and Pavlovian contingencies to resistance to change. I'll review the most interesting of them, beginning with experiments that manipulated the stimulus-reinforcer relation indirectly.

Serial schedules and resistance to change.

The first relevant experiment, in 1984, arranged serial schedules where stimuli signaling two different reinforcer rates are presented in 1-2 order, over and over, with a time out in between pairs. The purpose is to compare resistance to change in the first segments with identical response-reinforcer contingencies that are followed by second segments with different stimulus-reinforcer relations. Figure 5.1 shows how serial schedules operate. Serial schedules for operant behavior resemble Pavlovian serial conditioning, where a conditional stimulus (CS1) is followed by a second conditional stimulus (CS2) and then by the unconditional stimulus (US).[1]

The experiment arranged identical variable-interval (VI) schedules of food reinforcement in the first segments of

95

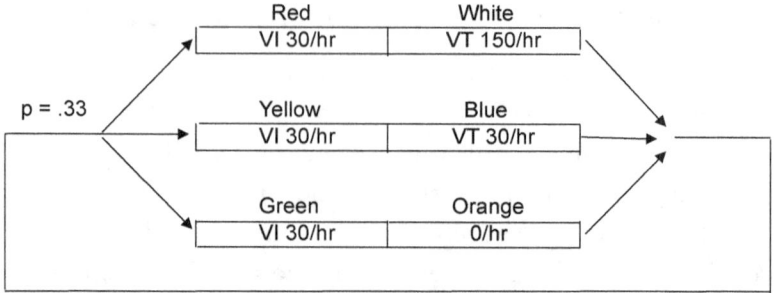

Figure 5.1. A diagram of three-component serial schedules arranged on three pecking keys, where the first segment in each component provides food reinforcers on identical VI 2-min schedules (30 reinforcers/hr) and the second segment arranges different rates of food presentation on variable-time (VT) schedules. Redrawn from Nevin (1984).

three serial schedules, presented successively on the three keys of the pigeon chamber, with different schedules of free food presentation (technically known as variable-time or VT schedules) in the second segments. Specifically, the schedules were VI 120 s (30/hr) in the first segments, and VT 24 s (150/hr), VT 120 s (30/hr), and extinction (0/hr) in the second segments. The question is how the second-segment schedule would influence first-segment response rates and their resistance to change, tested by prefeeding and by extinction after establishing stable baseline performances.

Figure 5.2 summarizes the average data. The upper panel shows that baseline response rates in the first segment were inversely related to the rate of food presentation in the second segment – an effect known as following-schedule contrast after it was first identified by Ben Williams at UCSD in 1979. However, the lower panel shows that resistance to change, measured as p_w, was directly related to the rate of food presentation in the second segment, in exact opposition to baseline response rate – clear evidence that response rate and

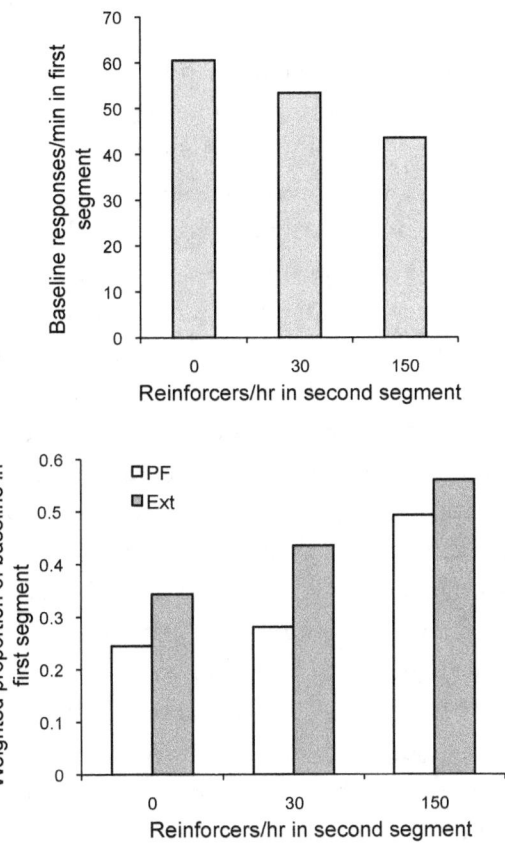

Figure 5.2. The upper panel shows average baseline response rates in the first segment of multiple serial schedules with different rates of response-independent reinforcement in the second segment. The lower panel shows resistance to prefeeding (PF) and to extinction (Ext) as weighted proportions of baseline. Redrawn from data of Nevin (1984).

resistance to change were separately determined aspects of behavior in this preparation. Interestingly, Williams reported a similar experiment in 1991 and observed preference for the first segment that preceded the richer second segment, in accord with resistance to change but not with baseline response rate.[2] Chapter 4 has already suggested a strong correlation between resistance to change and preference, and these studies provide another example.

Because of the similarity of the serial-schedule paradigm to Pavlovian serial conditioning, and because there was no response-reinforcer contingency on key pecking to produce the second segment or food in that segment, I argued that resistance to change was determined by a Pavlovian process – the stimulus-reinforcer contingencies. But the experiment did not compare response-contingent with noncontingent transitions. In 1987, Larry Smith, Jean Roberts – both graduate students at UNH – and I explored the role of operant contingencies in serial schedules. The basic question was whether response-contingent reinforcement strengthens operant behavior, in the sense of increasing resistance to change, just as it increases response rate (by the definition of reinforcement – see Chapter 2).[3]

We did two experiments to address this deliberately challenging question. In the first, we arranged a two-component multiple schedule with either response-contingent or noncontingent transitions from the first segment, with VI 180 s (20 reinforcers/hr), to the second segment, with VI 36 s (100 reinforcers/hr). First-segment response rates were higher in the contingent-transition component, showing that access to the second segment acted as a reinforcer in the conventional sense. However, there was no consistent difference in first-segment resistance to prefeeding or extinction, suggesting that

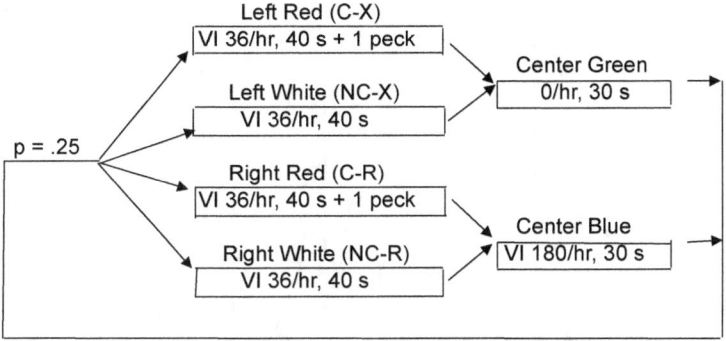

Figure 5.3. A diagram of four-component multiple serial schedules with their first segments arranged on the left and right side keys and their second segments on the center key of a three-key pigeon chamber. See text for explanation; based on Nevin et al. (1987).

reinforcing a response did not strengthen that response in the sense of increasing its persistence.

In our second experiment, we arranged four multiple-schedule components, each of which was a serial schedule with or without peck-contingent transitions from the first to the second segment. The first segments were always VI 100 s (36/hr), and the second segments were either VI 20 s (180/hr) or extinction (0/hr). In one pair of serial schedules, transitions from the first to the second segment were contingent on a key peck, so first-segment responding produced both infrequent food and a signal for more frequent food (designated C-R) or for extinction (designated C-X). In the other pair, transitions were independent of pecking, and the components are designated NC-R and NC-X. This admittedly complicated procedure is diagramed in Figure 5.3.

The average results are summarized in Figure 5.4.

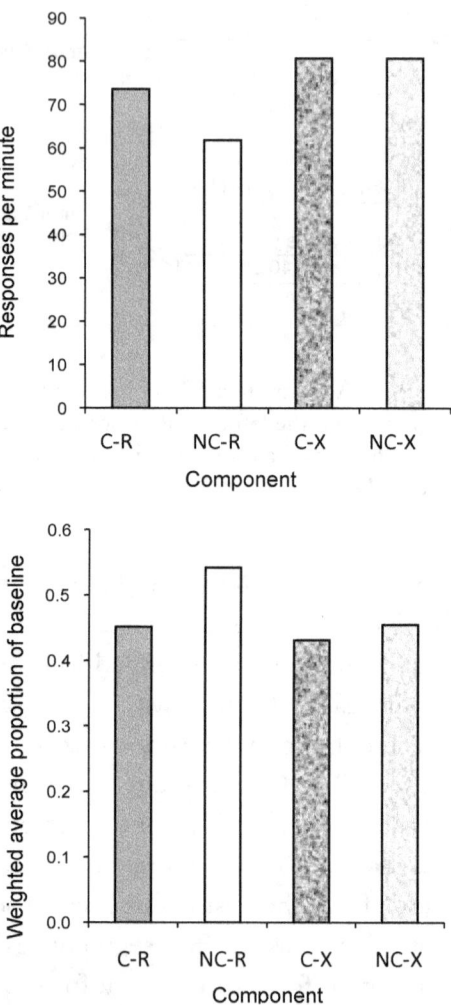

Figure 5.4. Upper panel: average baseline response rates in the first segments of multiple serial schedules that are followed by more frequent VI reinforcement (R) or by extinction (X) in the second segments, where the transition is either response-contingent (C) or noncontingent (NC). Lower panel: resistance to extinction in the first segments described above. Redrawn from data of Nevin et al. (1987).

The differences were not huge but they were statistically reliable. Baseline response rates were higher in C-R than in NC-R, showing once again that the contingent production of a signal for more frequent reinforcement was in fact a reinforcer in the traditional sense. Also, baseline response rates were higher in C-X and NC-X than in C-R and NC-R, replicating the following-schedule contrast effect in my 1984 experiment and in Williams's work. The data on resistance to extinction, measured as p_w, were generally opposite. Most interesting, resistance to extinction was reliably greater for NC-R than for C-R, suggesting that although response-contingent signals for frequent food increased response rate relative to noncontingent signals, the contingency may actually have weakened responding in terms of its resistance to extinction. Also, resistance to extinction was reliably greater in NC-R than in NC-X, replicating my 1984 result. Again, it appeared that the Pavlovian stimulus-reinforcer relation between signals and food was the major determiner of resistance to change, and there was no evidence that the operant contingency between first-segment pecking and onset of the second segment strengthened responding.

The effects of reinforcement context

Another indirect approach to the role of Pavlovian stimulus-reinforcer contingencies pitted two quite different accounts of response rate and resistance to change against each other. The basic idea developed from Richard Herrnstein's widely applicable, and widely accepted, account of response rate on VI schedules. As I showed in Chapter 3, his fundamental equation, expanded to account for multiple-schedule data, gave an excellent account of the ICI food data of my 1974 Experiment 1, which I interpreted

Table 5.1 Illustrative calculations of response rates and proportions of baseline predicted by Equation 5.1 in a multiple schedule component with 60 reinforcers per hr (r1) and either 300/hr or 10/hr (r2) in an alternated component, arranged in successive conditions A and B, with k = 100, m = 0.5, and r_0 = 10 (baseline) or 100 (disruption). Based on Nevin (1992).

Baseline	r_1	r_2	r_0	B_1	
Cond A	60	300	10	27.3	
Cond B	60	10	10	80.0	
Disruption					Prop. BL
Cond A	60	300	100	19.4	0.71
Cond B	60	10	100	36.4	0.45

quite differently in relation to resistance to change. Here's Herrnstein's expression for multiple schedules, written for one component only:

$$B_1 = kr_1/(r_1+mr_2+r_0),\qquad(5.1)$$

where B_1 represents baseline response rate in Component 1, k is the asymptotic response rate as the reinforcer rate r_1 becomes indefinitely large, r_2 is the reinforcer rate in the alternated Component 2, m is a parameter characterizing the sensitivity of B_1 to r_2, and r_0 is the rate of unspecified reinforcers. Any disruptor that reduces response rate while the component schedules remain unchanged must appear, in this equation, as an increase in the value of r_0. Moreover, the larger the value of r_2, the smaller will be the impact of a given increase in r_0. Sample calculations illustrating this implication of Equation 5.1 appear in Table 5.1.

In this illustration, the increase in baseline response rate B_1 between Conditions A and B, when r_2 decreases from

300 to 10/hr with r_1 constant, is an example of behavioral contrast – a common finding first identified by George Reynolds at Harvard in 1961. Equation 5.1 correctly predicts behavioral contrast in that steady-state response rate in the constant component must be inversely related to r_2. In addition, that equation predicts that when r_0 increases, resistance to change (expressed as a proportion of baseline) is directly related to r_2. Readers may wish to check this for themselves with other values of the reinforcer rates and parameters in Equation 5.1.

Now consider an alternative prediction based on the notion that resistance to change depends on the Pavlovian stimulus-reinforcer contingency. In 1981, John Gibbon, a fellow graduate student and later a colleague at Columbia, showed that an effective way to characterize the strength of the Pavlovian stimulus-reinforcer contingency in autoshaping (see Chapter 2) is to express the reinforcer rate in the presence of a stimulus relative to the overall average reinforcer rate in a session.[4]

Applying his suggestion to multiple schedules shown in Table 5.1, the stimulus-reinforcer contingency in Component 1 is weaker when r_2 – and hence the overall session reinforcer rate – is greater. To see this, consider Conditions A and B, where the session average reinforcer rate (assuming the ICI = 0) is (60+300)/2 = 180/hr in Condition A, and (60+10)/2 = 35/hr in Condition B. Thus, r_1 relative to the session average is 60/180 = 0.33 in Condition A and 60/35 = 1.71 in Condition B. Moreover, when the session average reinforcer rate is reduced by increasing the intercomponent interval (ICI), the Pavlovian contingency ratio increases further and resistance to change should increase in both components. If resistance to change depends directly on the stimulus-reinforcer contingency, the prediction is that resistance to change in Component 1 will be inversely related to r_2 – the opposite of the prediction generated from Herrnstein's Equation 5.1 for multiple schedules. [I note here that in general, science progresses most rapidly when experiments can distinguish between competing predictions that go in opposite directions, rather than merely confirming the presence of an effect in the direction predicted by one theory.]

In 1992, I published the results of two experiment suggested by the argument above, with a VI 1-minute (60/hr) schedule in Component 1 and with either VI 12-second (300/hr) or a VI 6-minute (10/hr) schedule in Component 2. Resistance to change was evaluated by prefeeding and by extinction after performance stabilized. In Experiment 1, the ICI was short (2 seconds) and in Experiment 2, it was long (2 minutes). Baseline response rates are presented in the left panel of Figure 5.5, and the resistance-to-change results are summarized as p_w in the middle and right panels.

In Experiment 1, there was a large contrast effect on baseline response rates in Component 1 – that is, response rate in the constant 60/hr component was higher when the alternated component reinforcer rate was 10/hr than when it was 300/hr, as predicted by Equation 5.1. Likewise, resistance to prefeeding and to extinction were reliably greater when the alternated schedule was 10/hr than when it was 300/hr, contrary to prediction by Equation 5.1. In Experiment 2, with a much longer ICI, the contrast effect was sharply attenuated – consistent with Herrnstein's account, where m would be expected to decrease when the ICI was increased. Likewise, differences between components in resistance to prefeeding and to extinction were reduced but, on average, were contrary to prediction by Equation 5.1. Overall, then, the results for

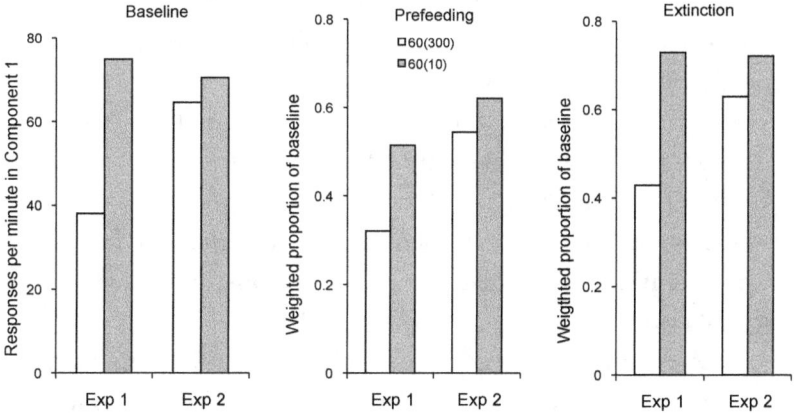

Figure 5.5. The left panel presents average baseline response rates in a multiple-schedule component with VI 60/hr, where the alternated component was either VI 300/hr or VI 10/hr. The ICI was 2 s in Experiment 1 and 2 min in Experiment 2. The center and right panels show the weighted proportions of baseline during prefeeding and extinction. Redrawn from data of Nevin (1992).

resistance to change are at least ordinally consistent with a Pavlovian stimulus-reinforcer interpretation but opposite to the predictions of Herrnstein's 1970 formulation.[5]

Since 1970, several analyses have challenged the particulars of Equation 5.1, but the same ordinal prediction follows from all of the alternatives that have been suggested. Evidently the effects of the Pavlovian contingency that is inherent in multiple schedules cannot be captured easily by accounts based on the matching law and its derivatives.

Randy Grace and I tried to repeat the 1992 study in a procedure designed to permit comparisons of different contexts within sessions rather than between successive conditions. We arranged two blocks of components on the left and right keys, one with VI 40 reinforcers/hr alternating with VI 160/hr, and the other with VI 40/hr alternating with VI 10/hr; the blocks were separated by 5 min blackout periods. We failed to replicate the effects of the alternative component on resistance to prefeeding in the constant component, although we did replicate the effects of extinction. Given these mixed findings, it really isn't clear whether we actually succeeded in defining two separate local contexts based on key location, or whether the entire experimental session, blackouts and all, constituted a single overall context.[6]

Given this uncertain state of affairs, and the importance of evaluating the role of the Pavlovian contingency versus Herrnstein's 1970 version of the law of effect, Randy, Ant McLean, and I replicated the 1992 study with eight pigeons in two conditions. In Component 1, the schedule was always VI 40/hr, and in the alternated Component 2, the schedule was either VI 200/hr or VI 6.67/hr. The order of exposure to the alternated component schedules was fully counterbalanced across subjects, thus removing a potential concern about my 1992 data. We repeated the resistance tests with prefeeding and extinction in each condition.[7]

Because the experiment was also designed to test a novel prediction about extinction, I will save the full story for Chapter 7, which considers a number of issues related to the effects of eliminating reinforcers. Here I will simply note that the prefeeding results were absolutely solid: All eight pigeons exhibited greater resistance to prefeeding in the condition where the constant 40/hr component alternated with the leaner alternative than in the condition with the richer alternative. Thus, we replicated the main finding from 1992: Resistance to change depends inversely on the reinforcer rate in the alternated component (see also Chapter 4).

In a separate review article in 1992, I suggested that

an appropriate expression for behavioral mass is $(r_s/r_a)^b$, where r_s is the reinforcer rate in a schedule component and r_a is the overall average reinforcer rate in an experimental session. As explained above, increasing the reinforcer rate in an alternative component increases the value of r_a, thus decreasing the value of r_s/r_a and hence reducing resistance to change. Accordingly, the full expression for resistance to change is:

$$\log(B_x/B_o) = -x/((r_s/r_a)^b \qquad (5.2)$$

The exponent b characterizes the sensitivity of resistance to change to reinforcer rate in a component relative to that in the session as a whole; when evaluated by fitting a lot of experimental data, its value ranges from about 0.3 to 0.7. Many data sets suggest a value of about 0.5, so that's the value we use when predicting resistance to change in a new experiment. Note that in standard two-component multiple schedules, r_a is the same for both components, and its value will be absorbed into the disruptor x. When comparisons are made between conditions with different values of r_a, however, the full expression must be used.[8]

Before we leave these indirect approaches to identifying stimulus-reinforcer relations as determiners of resistance to change, note again that response-reinforcer contingencies were the same in the constant-VI component, and the ordering of baseline response rates (left panel of figure 5.5) agreed with the ordering of resistance to change (center and right panels). By contrast, the ordering of response rates in the first segments in my 1984 serial-schedule study, which also had the same VI contingencies, was exactly opposite to the ordering of resistance to change (Fig. 5.3). Although these cross-experiment comparisons suggest that resistance to change depends on stimulus-reinforcer relations and not on baseline response rates when reinforcer rates and response-reinforcer contingencies are the same, more direct evidence is needed to make a stronger case.

Effects of added reinforcers

The most direct way to change the stimulus-reinforcer relation in a multiple schedule is, quite simply, to add alternative reinforcers to one of two otherwise identical components. The first study based on this approach was published in collaboration with Rick Shull and his students Mary Tota and Richard Torquato at UNC Greensboro; the collaboration arose from a happy convergence of independent interests.

In 1988, I had done an experiment that arranged a two-component multiple schedule with variable-interval (VI) 1-minute schedules in both components and, in successive conditions, a variable-time (VT) 30-second or a VT 15-second schedule running concurrently and delivering free food in one of those components, hereafter VI+VT. Thus, the response-reinforcer contingency was stronger in the VI-only component because reinforcers could be obtained only by responding. However, the stimulus-reinforcer relation was stronger in the VI+VT component because the component stimulus signaled more frequent reinforcers (see Chapter 2).

I evaluated resistance to prefeeding and resistance to extinction in each condition. Figure 5.6 presents the average data for Condition 2, with VT 30-s food (120/hr) in the VI+VT component, for baseline and for resistance to change. The left panel presents response rates determined during baseline, and the right panel presents weighted proportions

108

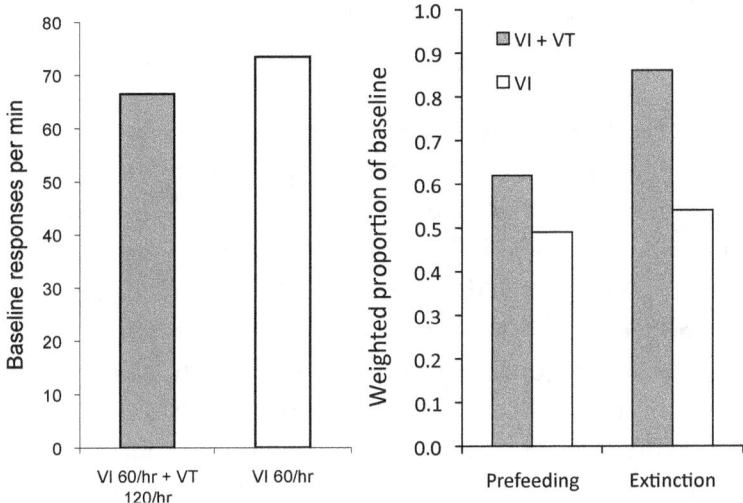

Figure 5.6. The left panel shows average baseline response rates in the components of multiple VI 1-min, VI 1-min schedules with 120 response-independent food presentations per hour added to the VI+VT component. The right panel shows weighted proportions of baseline when responding was disrupted by prefeeding or by extinction. Redrawn from data of Nevin et al. (1990)

of baseline during 5 sessions of prefeeding and, after baseline recovery, 7 sessions of extinction. Similar results were obtained in Condition 3, with VT 15-s food (240/hr) in the VI+VT component. Overall, response rate was lower but resistance to change was greater in the VI+VT component. [Note that the experiment by Shahan and Burke on alcohol reinforcers and alternative reinforcers, described in Chapter 1, has exactly the same structure and gave the same results as this experiment. The effect of added VT reinforcers on resistance to change has been replicated frequently with several species including goldfish and humans (see below) so it has substantial generality.[9] In fact, most of these studies have obtained stronger effects than my original experiment.]

I described these results to Rick Shull at a professional meeting, and he told me that he and his students had done something similar, albeit with a quite different method for adding reinforcers into a multiple-schedule component. Their experiment arranged for the equivalent of the added VT reinforcers in my experiment (Figure 5.6) to be delivered for pecking a second key. More specifically, they arranged a three-component multiple schedule on two pecking keys. In Component A, both keys were lighted green and pecking the right key was reinforced 15 times per hour, while pecking the left key was reinforced 45 times per hour, both according to VI schedules, for a total of 60 reinforcers per hour. (This is a concurrent VI VI schedule as described in Chapter 3.) In Component B, both keys were lighted red and pecking the right key was reinforced 15 times per hour (as in Component A) while left-key pecks were never reinforced. In Component C, both keys were lighted white and pecking the right key was reinforced 60 times per hour while left-key pecks were never reinforced, giving the same total reinforcement as in Component A. Note that Components A (right 15/hr + left 45/hr) and B (right 15/hr only) are analogous to VI+VT and VI-only components in my study. Therefore, if the stimulus-reinforcer relation is the critical determiner of resistance to change, right-key responding should be more resistant to change in Component A than in Component B because green keys signal 60 reinforcers/hr whereas red keys signal only 15 reinforcers/hr. Note also that the same total reinforcement (60/hr) was signaled by green keys in Component A and white keys in Component C. Therefore, right-key responding should be equally resistant to change in Components A and C despite the fact that right-key pecking was reinforced four times more often in Component C.

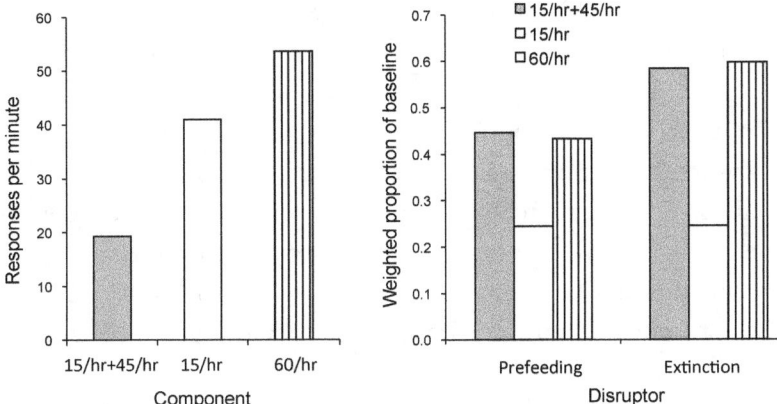

Figure 5.7. The left panel shows average baseline response rates on the right key in Components A (VI 15/hr plus VI 45/hr on the left key), B (VI 15/hr) and C (VI 60/hr). The right panel shows the weighted proportions of baseline during prefeeding and extinction. Redrawn from data of Nevin et al. (1990).

As shown in Figure 5.7, baseline response rates on the right key were highest in Component C (60/hr+extinction) and lowest in Component A (15/hr+45/hr), whereas resistance to change was virtually identical (on average) in Components A and C, with both being greater than in Component B (15/hr+extinction). This is strong evidence that the overall reinforcer rate correlated with component stimuli determines resistance to change independently of response rate. The results also resolve a problem: how to interpret VT food during baseline training in my Experiment 1. Perhaps some VT reinforcers that happened by chance to occur just after a key peck were indistinguishable, for the pigeon, from VI reinforcers. If so, the effective VI schedule in the VI+VT component would be richer than in the VI-only component, thus accounting for the greater resistance to change in the VI+VT component as a result of confusion

111

between VI and VT reinforcers. But Shull and his students obtained the same result even though the equivalent of the VT reinforcers were obtained on a second key according to a concurrent VI schedule, and the pigeons' overall choices between keys approximately equaled the overall allocation of reinforcers (i.e., matching – Equation 3.1), so confusion could be ruled out. We combined our separate studies into a single article that has been cited frequently in the applied as well as experimental literatures; the process of writing and revising, with each of us contributing different ways of presenting the data, was great fun.[10]

Applications with human participants

At about the same time as my encounter with Rick Shull, I had also described my finding of greater resistance to change in a component with added VT reinforcers to Bud Mace, and he and his colleagues set to work at once. First, they replicated the finding of greater resistance to change in the richer of two VI schedule components with adult residents of a group home (see Chapter 3). Then, they replicated the effects of added reinforcers in one component in a close analog to the pigeon study with VI versus VI+VT, described above. Their basic procedure was as described in Chapter 3, and the same two group-home residents were asked to perform the same sorting task. If they were sorting red utensils, they received popcorn or coffee according to a VI 60-s schedule, and if they were sorting green utensils, they received popcorn or coffee on the same VI schedule and also received additional popcorn or coffee, regardless of whether they were sorting or not, on a VT 30-s schedule. After sorting rates became stable, performance was disrupted by turning on an MTV show. Both subjects had lower sorting rates in the added-VT component, and their sorting rates were more resistant to distraction by the MTV show in that component. Individual data are presented in Figure 5.8.[11] Note that the effects of added VT reinforcers are even clearer than for the pigeon data presented in Figure 5.5. Because pigeons' key pecking can be established and maintained by the Pavlovian autoshaping procedure (see Chapter 2), the extension of the basic finding to humans with an arbitrary response (sorting) is especially important.

Mace's results were repeated by Steven Cohen in an extension of his study described in Chapter 3. He arranged a VT schedule of points as added reinforcers in one component of a multiple VI VI schedule where students typed words displayed on a computer monitor, and obtained a similar increase in resistance to distraction by a "Where's Waldo" puzzle book. Like sorting, typing is an arbitrary response that is not amenable to autoshaping, and again it appears that the stimulus-reinforcer relation determines resistance to change.

A further extension of this line of work to humans, and to a very different sort of response, was described by Mary Tota-Faucette in her doctoral dissertation at UNC-Greensboro. She explored the effects of added reinforcers on the persistence of muscle relaxation in children. She selected this as her target response for several reasons. First, relaxation is not a discrete, overt response like pressing a key, and because it is not easy to identify or control one's level of relaxation, it is less likely to be influenced by all the factors that complicate research with humans such as self-instructions based on what the subject believes the experimenter's desired outcome to be. Second, relaxation can be influenced by biofeedback – an external cue, such as the pitch of a tone,

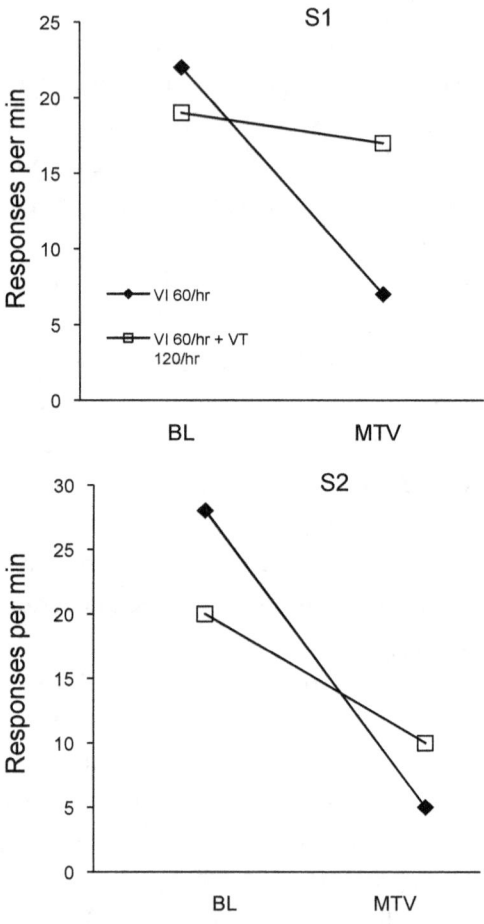

Figure 5.8. Rates of sorting utensils for two group-home residents in multiple VI, VI+VT schedules. Baseline sorting rates (BL) were disrupted by playing an MTV program. From Mace et al. (1990).

that is correlated with electrical signals picked up from the muscles (EMG) by an apparatus similar to that used to study rates and patterns of heartbeats (EKG). Biofeedback can be very effective in treating some headaches that result from muscle tension, but treatment effects usually diminish outside the biofeedback clinic. Therefore, Tota-Faucette was interested in whether the persistence of relaxation could be enhanced by added reinforcement in the same way as the simple overt repeated responses of nonhumans.[12]

Tota-Faucette studied normal children between 7 and 12 years old in a biofeedback lab where tension of the neck muscles could be monitored by a computer. She arranged that whenever the EMG signal indicating muscle tension went below a criterion, the child heard a feedback tone – arguably, a reinforcer for relaxing – in 30-second trials. (An alternative view is that relaxing is intrinsically reinforcing, and that the tone serves merely to define the response.) Trials were arranged as multiple-schedule components signaled by different colored lights. In both components, points were displayed on a counter for every 3 seconds that the tone remained on; in one component, free reinforcers – either points, or candy that could be eaten after the session – were also signaled at the end of a trial, regardless of whether the child had been relaxed or not. Points accumulated on the counter were exchanged for play dollars, which could be used to buy toys. The test of persistence was simply to turn off the tone – extinction – so there was no immediate feedback or other explicit consequences for relaxing; however, accumulated points and candy were given at end of the test sessions in order to keep the children engaged in the experiment.

During training, the children learned to lower their EMG levels, showing that the behavior of relaxing was reinforced

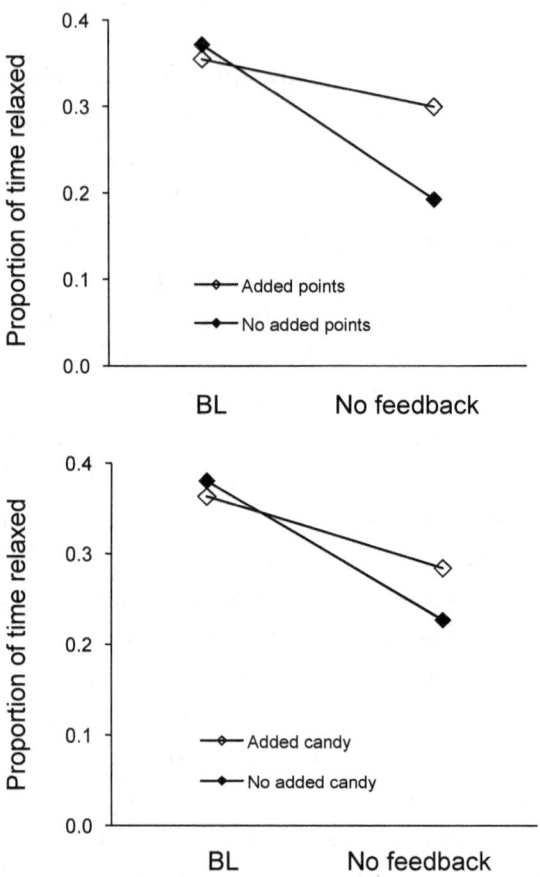

Figure 5.9. Proportions of time spent relaxed during baseline when feedback tones and points were presented, and when feedback was discontinued, as in extinction. The upper and lower panels show the results for conditions where one component included added points or candy, regardless of whether the subject was relaxed. Redrawn from data provided by Tota-Faucette (1991).

– i.e., made more probable – by sensory feedback and points, and in baseline, the proportion of time spent relaxed was similar in the two components. During extinction, EMG levels relative to their training baselines remained lower for longer times in the component with added points (same reinforcers, 11 of 12 children) or with added candy (different reinforcers, 9 of 11 children). The average results are shown in Figure 5.9.

These extinction test results not only generalize the effects of added reinforcers to a covert, continuous response (relaxation) in normal children, but also show that comparable enhancement of persistence can be obtained with added reinforcers that are qualitatively different from those explicitly arranged for relaxing.

The effects of added reinforcers that are qualitatively different from the ones produced by the measured response have been replicated several times. For example, Julie Grimes and Rick Shull at UNC Greensboro trained 12 rats in multiple schedules with identical VI schedules of food reinforcement. Sweetened condensed milk was presented independently of responding in one component, and resistance to extinction was evaluated over three sessions. For 11 of the 12 rats, response rates were higher in the food-only component but resistance to extinction was greater in the food plus milk component.[13] The study by Shahan and Burke described in Chapter 1, with alcohol reinforcers in both components and added VT food in one component, provides further confirmation of the results.

A lot of clinical interventions with participants who exhibit various forms of problem behavior use added reinforcers contingent upon some form of alternative behavior, rather than noncontingently on VT schedules, in order to increase the rate of desirable behavior while reducing the rate of problem behavior. In the procedure arranged by Shull and his students in our second experiment (Figure 5.7), Component A is known, in applied work, as Differential Reinforcement of Alternative Behavior (DRA). If right-key pecking represents some form of undesired problem behavior and left-key pecking represents desirable alternative behavior, arranging DRA in Component A during baseline training reduces problem behavior relative to Component B (no DRA) – a finding that has been confirmed repeatedly in clinical applications as well as experimental settings. But although DRA is effective in the steady state (compare Components A and B in the left panel of Figure 5.7), it also increases resistance to change (compare Components A and B in the right panel of Figure 5.7). If this result generalizes to clinical settings, the increased persistence of problem behavior as a byproduct of reinforcing desirable behavior is, to say the least, problematic.

And the problem is not hypothetical. Bud Mace and his colleagues have obtained this outcome in a clinical setting with three children who exhibited aggressive and disruptive problem behavior such as hair-pulling, food-stealing, and self-injury. For example, Andy was a 7-year-old boy diagnosed with autism who engaged in hair-pulling. During baseline determinations (BL), Andy received verbal reprimands for hair-pulling, which evidently functioned as reinforcers (even a reprimand is probably better than no attention at all). During DRA, reprimands for hair-pulling continued, and in addition, Andy was prompted to play with toys and received praise for doing so. As shown in Figure 5.10, Andy's hair-pulling rate decreased substantially relative to baseline. During extinction, hair-pulling was blocked and all reinforcers (including

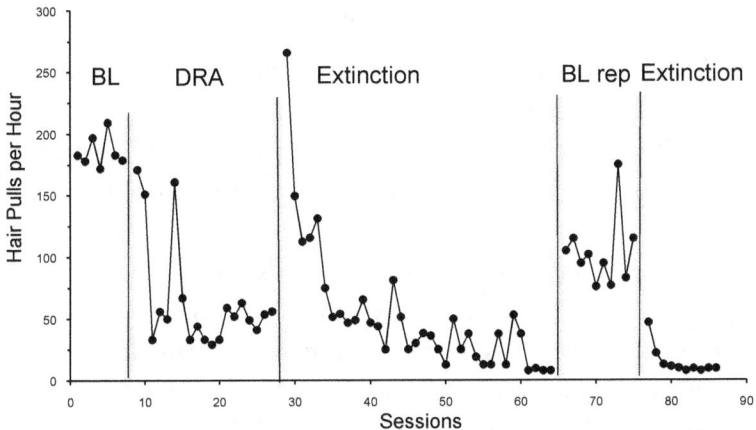

Figure 5.10. Hair pulling by Andy in an initial baseline determination, treatment with DRA, and then a post-DRA extinction test, followed by a repeat determination of baseline before a final extinction test without intervening DRA treatment. Reproduced from Mace et al. (2010) by permission of John Wiley & Sons, Inc..

reprimands) were withheld. Nevertheless, the rate of hair-pulling attempts increased sharply at first, to a level well above baseline, and then persisted at moderate levels for at least 20 sessions. After baseline conditions were restored (BL rep), extinction was repeated and hair-pulling decreased more rapidly and to lower levels than when extinction followed DRA. Similar data were obtained with two other participants who experienced DRA after an initial baseline and extinction sequence, ruling out possible order effects.[13]

Evidently, DRA can be quite effective in reducing the rate of problem behavior in a clinical setting, but it can also have the counter-therapeutic side effect of increasing the persistence of that behavior when DRA is discontinued, confirming the implications of the pigeon data of Figure 5.7. We will return to this problem in Chapter 9.

Summary

Here's a summary of the main conclusions suggested by the research reviewed to this point.

1. Discriminated free-operant behavior has two separable dimensions: Steady-state response rate and resistance to change.

2. Steady-state response rate depends on operant response-reinforcer contingencies, including relative reinforcement for a designated response as specified by Herrnstein's equations, whereas resistance to change is independent of response rate and depends instead on Pavlovian stimulus-reinforcer contingencies.

3. Resistance to change is an increasing function of the rate or amount of reinforcement signaled by a discriminative stimulus relative to the overall reinforcer rate in the context.

4. In the metaphor of behavioral momentum, steady-state response rate is analogous to the velocity of a moving object, and resistance to change measures the analog of that object's mass.

5. Preference for a discriminative stimulus and resistance to change of responding in the presence of that stimulus are highly correlated, providing convergent measurement of the strength, value, or behavioral mass of discriminated operant behavior.

Taken together, these conclusions constitute the essence of what has come to be known as Behavioral Momentum Theory. The next chapter will consider various empirical challenges to these statements.

Chapter 6

Challenges to Behavioral Momentum Theory

There is an appealing simplicity to Conclusions 2 and 3 at the end of Chapter 5, which can be restated, "In the momentum metaphor, velocity is Skinnerian and mass is Pavlovian." This catchy line was first suggested by Sherman Roberts, with whom I worked at the Cambridge Center for Behavioral Studies in 1991, and I used it in various lectures and presentations to professional audiences during the 1990s. However, there are some exceptions to the proposition that Pavlovian stimulus-reinforcer relations are the only determiners of resistance to change – some of which I knew about even while giving my simplified take-home message. Moreover, I have coauthored several articles that challenge my own generalization. Let's start by looking at some studies showing that a difference in stimulus-reinforcer relations between components is not necessary to establish a difference in resistance to change. Some of the material here – and in Chapter 5 – has recently appeared in a handbook chapter written by Andy Craig and Amy Odum at USU, who invited me to participate in its preparation.[1]

121

Different operant contingencies with equated reinforcer rates

If resistance to change depends solely on Pavlovian stimulus-reinforcer relations, there should be no difference in resistance to change between multiple-schedule components when stimulus-reinforcer relations are the same. To the contrary, several studies have found that when obtained reinforcer rates are matched between components but response-reinforcer contingencies differ between components, high response rates are generally less resistant to any of a variety of disruptors than low response rates. A 1968 study by Derek Blackman provides an example.[2] Six rats were trained in multiple schedules with identical VI schedules of food reinforcement but different contingencies on response rate in the components. For example, in Component A, for Rat 1, only those responses occurring within 0.2 s of the previous response were reinforced (differential reinforcement of high rate, DRH); in Component B, only those responses that were spaced between 1.5 and 3.0 s were reinforced (a pacing schedule). As a result, response rate in Component A was about double that in Component B, even though obtained reinforcer rates were essentially identical. When a 1-min tone signaling an unavoidable shock was presented in the middle of each 8-min component, responding was suppressed much more, relative to its pre-tone baseline, in Component A (high-rate DRH) than in Component B (low-rate pacing). Similar results were obtained with 5 other rats with varying DRH and pacing requirements. Thus, low-rate responding was more resistant than high-rate responding to the disruptive effects of signaled shock.[2]

In the same study, six other rats were trained with

identical DRH or pacing requirements in Components A and B but with different reinforcer rates. For example, for Rat 8, responses that were spaced between 1.5 and 3.0 s were reinforced in both Components A and B (as in Component B for Rat 1). However, the reinforcers were more frequent in Component A. Response rates in Components A and B were essentially identical, but responding was less suppressed by signaled shock in Component A. The same results were obtained with 5 other rats with various DRH and pacing schedules. Evidently, when stimulus-reinforcer relations are the same in two components, resistance to change depends on the response rate established by response-reinforcer contingencies, but when response-reinforcer contingencies are the same, resistance to change depends on stimulus-reinforcer relations.

Following Blackman, I had attempted to pit response rate against reinforcer rate as determiners of resistance to change in the last experiment reported in my 1974 study of response strength in multiple schedules.[3] In one condition, I arranged a DRH contingency in a component with a VI 3-min schedule, and a DRL contingency in an alternated component with a VI 1-min schedule; in a second condition, the pairing of contingencies and reinforcer rates was reversed.

The effects of reinforcer rate were clear: In all comparisons, resistance to change was greater in the component with the higher reinforcer rate, regardless of the baseline rates established by DRL or DRH contingencies, confirming that aspect of Blackman's study. When the data were compared across conditions with the same reinforcer rates, responding was substantially more resistant to ICI food in the DRL component in five of eight comparisons, and more resistant to extinction in three of eight comparisons; the remaining comparisons were ambiguous. Nevertheless, I allowed myself to construe these admittedly weak results as generally agreeing with Blackman's findings.

My tentative conclusion was supported in 1989 by Andy Lattal, who trained pigeons on VI schedules with tandem FR (effectively, DRH) or differential reinforcement of low rate (DRL) contingencies that produced high *vs* low response rates with equated reinforcer rates in multiple-schedule components. When responding was disrupted by ICI food, varied over three values, low-rate responding was consistently more resistant to change.[4]

However, in a 1983 study with pigeons, Steve Fath and his colleagues failed to find a difference in resistance to change between components with high-rate and low-rate pacing contingencies superimposed on identical VI schedules. Although their pigeons' baseline response rates differed by more than a factor of 2, there were no consistent differences in resistance to change relative to baseline when responding was disrupted by ICI food in a series of single test sessions, with the duration of ICI food varied over successive resistance tests separated by baseline redeterminations.[5]

Overall, this mixture of findings led me to believe that Blackman's and Lattal's findings, and my own DRL *vs* DRH data from 1974, were not decisive against the principle that resistance to change was independent of response-reinforcer contingencies. The basic reason is that, in all these studies, the high- and low-rate performances were qualitatively different. A DRH contingency superimposed on a VI schedule establishes steady, rapid responding, whereas a low-rate pacing or DRL contingency establishes a pause-then-respond pattern. Therefore, comparing changes in the measured

124

rates of the designated response would be like comparing changes in the running speeds of hares and tortoises when tempted by a chance to relax in the shade: The hare might give in easily while the tortoise just keeps lumbering along. Accordingly, I discounted these admittedly inconsistent data as serious challenges to the role of the stimulus-reinforcer relation as the determiner of resistance to change.

In a comment on the Law of Effect article that Randy Grace and I published in 2000, Marc Branch proposed that a comparison between variable-ratio (VR) and variable-interval (VI) schedules with equated reinforcer rates could provide a stronger test of the role of stimulus-reinforcer relations, because VR and VI both maintain fairly steady responding but at quite different average rates. Randy, Ant McLean, Ant's student Shasta Holland, and I took up Branch's challenge. In one experiment, we arranged random-ratio (RR) schedules, which are essentially like VR schedules in that they produce steady, rapid responding in one component, and random-interval (RI) schedules, which are essentially like VI schedules in that they produce steady lower-rate responding in the alternated component. We equated the obtained reinforcer rates by adjusting the RI schedule to equal the observed interval between reinforcers in the RR component in the preceding session, and found that the lower response rate in the RI component was generally more resistant to disruption than in the RR component. Moreover, the difference in resistance to change between components depended on individual baseline response rates before disruption: The higher the response rate in the RR component relative to that in the RI component, the greater the resistance to change in the RI component relative to the RR component.[6]

In a second experiment, we arranged VR and VI

125

schedules in the terminal links of concurrent chain schedules (see Chapter 4) with different reinforcer rates; in two conditions, the VR value was adjusted every few sessions so that the VR yielded the same obtained reinforcer rate as in the VI component. When reinforcer rates were similar, lower-rate VI responding was generally less disrupted by intercomponent food, extinction, and intercomponent food plus extinction than was high-rate VR responding. Moreover, the difference in resistance to change between components depended on individual differences in the baseline response rates in the same way as with RI and RR schedules. In summary, we confirmed Blackman's and Lattal's results: When reinforcer rates were the same in two multiple-schedule components, resistance to change was greater, relative to baseline, in the component with the lower response rate. Evidently, my attempt to explain away the earlier data was misguided, and response-reinforcer contingencies can affect resistance to change when stimulus-reinforcer relations in multiple schedules are the same between components.

Delay to reinforcement

When reinforcers are presented immediately after eligible responses, the rate of responding is usually higher than when unsignaled delays intervene between responses and reinforcers. Working with Ben Williams at UCSD, Matt Bell arranged multiple schedules with immediate or delayed reinforcers, adjusted to ensure equal overall reinforcer rates, and confirmed the expected difference in response rates. He then tested for differences in resistance to change and found that responding was more resistant to several different disruptors in the immediate-reinforcement component. He described his findings at a 1996 meeting where Randy Grace and I were in the audience, and all of us appreciated the difficulty posed for the notion that resistance to change was determined by Pavlovian contingencies: Because the delays from component onset to reinforcement were the same, stimulus-reinforcer relations were the same for immediate and delayed reinforcers, but resistance to change was reliably greater in the component with immediate reinforcement. Jed Schwendiman, a graduate student at UNH, and Randy and I confirmed Bell's results: Response rates were higher and resistance to prefeeding and to extinction were greater in the component with immediate reinforcement.[7]

Thus, we now have two lines of research that pose difficulties for a purely Pavlovian account of resistance to change when baseline reinforcer rates are equated. In general, low response rates are more resistant to change than high rates when different response-reinforcer contingencies are in effect. However, if the difference in response rates results from delayed versus immediate reinforcement – also a response-reinforcer contingency – the higher response rate maintained by immediate reinforcement is more resistant to change. What might these seemingly opposed findings have in common?

Response rate, reinforcer delay, and preference

Chapter 4 described the relation between resistance to change in multiple schedules (or terminal links) and preference in the initial links of concurrent chains. Nearly all the data came from experiments that varied the reinforcer rates or delays. However, there are several studies of preference between different response-reinforcer contingencies, and the response rates they maintain, with reinforcer rates equated between terminal links. In a 1968 study, Ed Fantino examined the effects of response-reinforcer contingencies. For one group of pigeons, he arranged a DRH requirement in one terminal link but no required response rate in the other; in a separate group, terminal links arranged DRL *vs* no requirement. Fantino found clear preference away from DRH, but no clear preference toward or away from DRL.[8] The preference away from a high-rate contingency might help to account for the relative ease with which high response rates are disrupted.

To explore this possibility, I followed up my 1974 Experiment 5 by arranging concurrent chains with VI DRH or VI DRL schedules in the terminal links, using the same DRH or DRL requirements and the same pigeons. Thus, pigeons could choose between components with equal rates of reinforcement but with required high or low response rates to obtain those reinforcers. I found evidence of stronger preference for DRL over DRH in the same pigeons that had previously shown greater resistance to ICI food and extinction with DRL, and published the findings in a 1979 review.[9]

Figure 6.1 presents my resistance to change data from 1974 plotted against the follow-up preference data for individual pigeons taken from my 1979 review chapter, with differential resistance to prefeeding and extinction shown as grey-filled or black triangles, respectively. The figure also shows individual resistance and preference data for all three disruptor conditions from the equated-reinforcement components from the VR-VI study described above. Differential resistance to ICI food, extinction, and the combination of these disruptors are represented as grey-

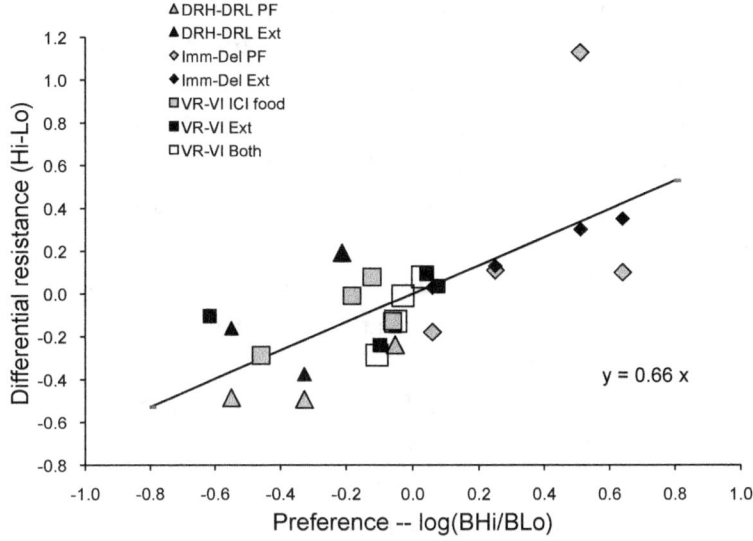

Figure 6.1. The relation between differential resistance to change in multiple schedule components with high-rate and low-rate contingencies and preference between terminal links with the same contingencies in concurrent chains. The data points are for individual pigeons in the studies by Nevin (1979, triangles); Grace et al. (2001, diamonds); and Nevin et al. (2001, squares). The relation between resistance and preference is similar to that displayed in Figure 4.4, but the slope is steeper.

filled, black, and white squares, respectively (group data on preference for VI over VR schedules are included in Figure 4.4).

We can also get resistance and preference data from the delayed *vs* immediate reinforcement study described above. Before conducting the evaluation of resistance to change, Randy, Jed, and I arranged concurrent chains with variable but equal overall delays to reinforcement, where reinforcers followed pecks after an unsignaled 3-second delay at the end of one terminal link or immediately after a peck in the other. The degree of preference varied between subjects, but all four gave evidence of preference for immediate reinforcement. Differential resistance is plotted against preference for individual subjects in Figure 6.1, where grey-filled and black diamonds represent prefeeding and extinction respectively. Overall, there is a strong positive correlation between differential resistance and preference that looks similar for delayed *vs* immediate and high *vs* low response rates, even though preference and resistance were measured in separate experimental conditions.

Although the critical differences between response-reinforcer contingencies that selectively reinforce higher or lower response rates and those that involve immediate or delayed reinforcement to maintain higher or lower response rates remain obscure, the correlation of differential resistance to change and preference looks pretty solid. Chapter 4 argued that resistance to change and preference could be interpreted as convergent measures of behavioral mass, so challenges to Pavlovian stimulus-reinforcer relations as determiners of resistance to change need not undermine the fundamental concepts of behavioral momentum – if the relation between preference and differential resistance holds up.

Limits to the preference-resistance relation

The linear relation between preference and resistance to change suggests that one is directly convertible into the other: Any factor that increases preference between two conditions should also increase the difference in resistance to change maintained by those two conditions, and vice versa. However, there is at least one exception. A number of concurrent-chains studies have demonstrated a large and robust preference for VI over FI when the average time between VI reinforcers is the same as the FI value. However, there is little evidence of a comparable difference in resistance to change: Charlotte Mandell failed to find any difference in resistance to satiation in multiple schedules, and Richard Mellon, working with Rick Shull and employing a similar multiple-chains paradigm, found only modest differences in initial-link resistance to satiation or extinction favoring the VI.[10] The FI-VI problem remains to be resolved.

Another exception arises when the initial-link schedules are varied. A number of studies have shown that preference between a given pair of terminal-link schedules increases systematically as the initial links get shorter. Chris Podlesnik, Corina Jimenez-Gomez, and Eric Thrailkill, studying with Tim Shahan at USU, reasoned that this so-called initial-link effect on preference should be accompanied by a corresponding increase in differential resistance, but obtained the expected relation only under a fairly narrow set of conditions. At the same time, they obtained a strong negative correlation between initial-link resistance to change and the ratio of terminal-link response rates, consistent with the suggestion above that response rates per se might affect relative strength or value.[11] All in all, the effects on preference and resistance to change of initial-link length, terminal-link schedule type, and response rates complicate the convergent measurement of behavioral mass proposed in Chapter 4.

Extremely different reinforcer rates

The role of Pavlovian contingencies in determining resistance to change has recently been challenged from the opposite direction. In 2012, Ant McLean completed a long-term study with two-component multiple VI VI schedules that covered a far greater range of reinforcer rate ratios

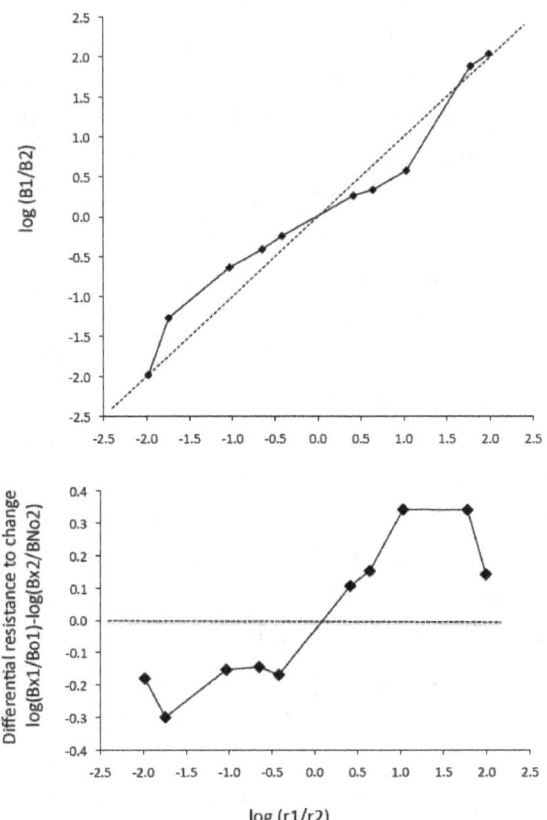

Figure 6.2. The upper panel displays the relation between the log ratio of response rates and the log ratio of reinforcer rates during baseline training over an unusually wide range (compare Figure 3.5). The lower panel displays the difference in resistance to prefeeding at each ratio of reinforcer rates. Note that as the baseline response-rate ratio approaches matching, differential resistance deviates toward 0 from the overall trend on the y-axis. Redrawn from data of McLean et al. (2012).

than any previous study. All of the multiple-schedule studies reviewed above arranged VI schedules with reinforcer rate ratios between 2:1 and 12:1; by contrast, Ant's experiment covered a four log-unit range from about 1:100 to 100:1. The major purpose of the study was to evaluate the relation between the ratios of response rates and reinforcer rates as expressed by the generalized matching law (Equation 3.3, Chapter 3), but resistance to prefeeding was evaluated at each reinforcer ratio as well.[12]

The upper panel of Figure 6.2 shows the relation between the logarithms of the ratio of responses and the ratio of reinforcers in McLean's multiple-schedule Components 1 and 2. Strict matching is implied by data that conform to the 45-degree dotted line (slope 1.0); note that the extreme data points approximate matching closely. When the data suggest a shallower slope, the result is termed undermatching. The slope is shallower than 1.0 over the range from +1 to -1 log units on the x-axis, which is the range of reinforcer ratios explored in nearly all previous research in which undermatching has been the usual outcome, as in the Reynolds and Shettleworth data displayed in Figure 3.5.

The lower panel of Figure 6.2 shows that resistance to prefeeding, tested after exposure to each reinforcer ratio, became less differentiated between rich and lean components at those extreme ratios. This is an unexpected difficulty for the notion that resistance to change depends on stimulus-reinforcer contingencies because the difference between components should be maximal at the extremes. McLean pointed out that when response ratios match reinforcer ratios, as at the extremes, it is necessarily true that the probability of reinforcement per response is the same in both components.

133

(To see this, write $B_1/B_2 = r_1/r_2$ – strict matching – and then rewrite as $r_1/B_1 = r_2/B_2$, where r/B is the proportion of reinforced responses, or probability of reinforcement for B.) Therefore, if probability of reinforcement per response determines resistance to change, rather than rate of reinforcement correlated with a stimulus, there should be little or no difference in resistance to change at extreme reinforcer ratios. Because there is some difference in resistance to change even at the most extreme reinforcer ratios, both rate of reinforcement and probability of reinforcement might combine in some way to determine resistance to change.

The differences in steady-state response rates may also play a role. At the extreme reinforcer ratios, response ratios are equally extreme, so if high response rates are less resistant to change than low response rates, as suggested above, the difference between response rates *per se* could modulate the relation between reinforcer rates and resistance to change. In any case, probability of reinforcement cannot be the whole story, because it cannot account for the data on resistance to change in a constant schedule component when the reinforcer rate in the alternated component was varied (see Chapter 5), nor can it account for the effects of delayed reinforcement on resistance to change described above. In both studies, resistance to change was greater in the component with the higher response rate, hence a lower probability of reinforcement.

In one way or another, the studies discussed above challenge the dependence of resistance to change on Pavlovian stimulus-reinforcer relations and the generality of the relation between preference and resistance to change. However, there is no obvious single principle that unifies all of these challenging results.

Resistance to change in single schedules

Virtually all laboratory research on resistance to change has arranged multiple schedules – most often, variable-interval (VI) schedules – because baseline response rates and resistance to change could be compared within subjects and sessions, and obtained reinforcer rates would be relatively unaffected by most disruptors (except, of course, for extinction, which is considered at length in Chapter 7). When different conditions of reinforcement are arranged in single schedules for entire sessions and compared across successive conditions, the usual positive relation between resistance to change and reinforcer rate may not be obtained. For example, with rats as subjects, Steven Cohen and his colleagues found that resistance to prefeeding was about the same for VI 30-s, VI 60-s, and VI 120-s schedules arranged singly, whereas resistance to prefeeding was directly related to reinforcer rate for fixed-interval (FI) 30-s and FI 120-s schedules arranged as multiple-schedule components. Similar ordinal differences (or lack thereof) were obtained with pigeons in FI and fixed-ratio (FR) schedules arranged singly or in multiple-schedule components.[13]

In 1998, Cohen suggested that the difference between resistance to change in single and multiple schedules arose from the frequency of alternating exposure to different reinforcer rates. He compared resistance to prefeeding after training with VI 30-s and VI 120-s schedules arranged singly in successive conditions (Part 1); in alternating days (Part 2); and in standard multiple schedules (Part 3). Distinctive stimuli accompanied the schedules throughout all three phases. As found by Cohen et al. (1993), resistance to prefeeding was about the same for both schedules in Part 1 but was greater for the richer component in Part 3. Interestingly, results for Part 2 depended on whether the schedule and accompanying stimulus were constant throughout each session or alternated with a different stimulus signaling extinction, thus defining a multiple VI Ext schedule. Subjects that experienced multiple VI Ext with the VI value alternating between rich and lean from day to day exhibited greater resistance to prefeeding with the richer schedule, suggesting that signaled reinforcement versus extinction defined differential stimulus-reinforcer relations.[14]

A recent study by Karen Lionello-DeNolf and Bill Dube compared the effects of added variable-time (VT) reinforcers (see Chapter 5) in single-schedule successive conditions and in multiple schedules with separate groups of children with various developmental disabilities. The schedules were VI 12 s plus VT 6 s or VI 12 s only, reinforcers were food items or tokens exchangeable for various preferred items, and responding was disrupted by presenting a different stimulus that signaled VI 8-s reinforcement for an alternative response concurrently with the target response. The results were clear: Responding was less disrupted in the VI+VT component for all six children trained and tested with multiple schedules, consistent with many previous findings, but the same ordering was observed with only two of six children experiencing the same schedules in successive conditions. Evidently, the difference between single and multiple schedules extends to translational settings and includes the effects of added noncontingent reinforcers.[15]

Thus, it appears that the direct relation between resistance to change and the rate of reinforcement in the presence of a component stimulus that is characteristic of multiple schedules may not be general to single schedules.

Note, however, that Mace and his colleagues repeated the usual effects of alternative reinforcers in a DRA treatment without distinctive external stimuli within sessions or between successive conditions (Figure 5.10). The central issue may be the definition of the context within which a discriminative stimulus and its accompanying schedule of reinforcement are experienced. In multiple schedules, a component is embedded within an experimental context that includes other components with different reinforcer rates, and we know from my 1992 study (and its subsequent replication) that resistance to change in a constant component depends inversely on the overall average reinforcer rate in the experimental context. In single schedules where environmental conditions are uniform throughout the session, the only stimulus that signals reinforcers is the experimental chamber, and the context is either undefined or identical to that given by the stimulus provided by the chamber. Both Cohen and Lionello-DeNolf and Dube provide thoughtful discussions of the differences between single and multiple schedules that are relevant to basic principles of resistance to change, and the resolution of the discrepancies reviewed here is vital for their application outside the laboratory.

Summary

The various problems, challenges, and limitations on momentum theory that the reader has struggled through in this chapter may suggest that resistance to change is so complexly determined as to defy any effort at theoretical integration. But let us not, as one says, lose sight of the forest because of the variety of trees within it. As we have seen, the resistance to change of discriminated operant behavior is directly related to the rate, amount, or immediacy of reinforcement in a number of different experimental arrangements, for subjects including goldfish, humans, pigeons, and rats; the humans include children and adults, some of whom have intellectual or developmental disabilities. Reinforcers have included biofeedback signals, points or tokens, and edibles for the humans, in addition to the usual food or water reinforcers used with nonhuman animals. That's a pretty broad domain of converging results, all instances of which are consistent with behavioral momentum theory. Until some more general principle comes along, I will stand by the conclusion that the relation between stimuli and reinforcers gives a good account of resistance to change.

Chapter 7

Extinction and Recovery

The conclusion of Chapter 6 summarized the effects of reinforcement rate, amount, or immediacy on resistance to change without listing the various disruptors that have been used in research on momentum in multiple schedules, so here they are. In the studies with nonhuman animals discussed or cited in the foregoing chapters, the list includes intercomponent (ICI) food, prefeeding or deprivation change, punishment, signaled shock, and response effort; with humans, distraction by stimuli such as TV or by competing activities such as puzzles have often been used. Intuitively, they are like external forces in physics applied while a body is in motion: They can be applied equally to both component performances while the component schedules continue to operate and make reinforcers available. The assumption of equality was essential for the analyses that were inspired by the momentum metaphor, including the suggestion that preference and resistance to change could provide converging estimation of the mass-like aspect of behavior traditionally termed response strength (Chapter 4). With few exceptions, response rate in the richer component was reliably more resistant to each of these disruptors.

In the learning literature, response strength is often measured as resistance to extinction. This is plausible: If responding continues for some time after reinforcement has been discontinued, that's evidence for strengthening by reinforcement during training. In terms of the momentum metaphor, however, extinction differs from external disruptors like ICI food in that, by definition, the component schedules that determine resistance to change are no longer operative; therefore, behavioral mass may diminish as extinction progresses. Moreover, the assumption of equality is dubious; terminating a component schedule with very frequent reinforcers is likely to be more disruptive than terminating a schedule that provides only a few reinforcers per hour. Let's start by reviewing some data, then consider the ways in which extinction may disrupt ongoing behavior, and go on to develop a quantitative model for the extinction process. Finally, we'll return to the question of whether behavioral mass decreases during extinction.

Replicating the PREE

Every student of the psychology of learning has been told (correctly) that operant behavior is more resistant to extinction after intermittent or partial reinforcement (PRF) than after continuous reinforcement (CRF), a result known as the partial-reinforcement extinction effect (PREE). The vast majority of experiments examining the PREE have employed rats as subjects in discrete-trial procedures where the rat runs down an alley, and the usual measure is response speed or latency within a trial, unlike the free-operant procedures employed in all the studies discussed above. Also, most studies have compared CRF and PRF conditions between independent groups rather than in multiple schedules that provide comparisons within individual subjects and sessions. Nevertheless, the PREE is a serious challenge to the generalization that more frequently reinforced responding is stronger –more resistant to change – because CRF necessarily provides a higher rate of reinforcement than any intermittent or partial schedule. In addition, the agreement between differential resistance and preference, summarized in Chapters 4 and 6, is violated by the PREE because CRF is preferred to PRF – an intuitively obvious result confirmed by Walter vom Saal in 1970.[1]

When a result appears to challenge an established theory, it's a good idea to try to repeat the result under the general conditions within which that the theory was developed. Therefore, to show that the PREE can be obtained in a discrete-trial version of within-subject multiple-schedule procedures of the sort used in the studies described in earlier chapters, I did a simple experiment in 1989.[2] In a two-key chamber, pigeons were trained to peck the left key when it was lighted white, and the right key when it was lighted red, mimicking multiple-schedule components. In irregular alternation, one key or the other was lighted after an intertrial interval (ITI) averaging 25 seconds; the key light turned off after a single key peck or after 5 seconds if no peck occurred. This is a discrete-trial procedure like many used in research on the PREE, but the dependent measure was the probability of response given a trial rather than latency or speed of response. Pecks on left, white-key trials were always reinforced (CRF), and pecks on right, red-key trials were reinforced with probability 0.25 (PRF). After 55 training sessions, food reinforcement was discontinued for 12 sessions

141

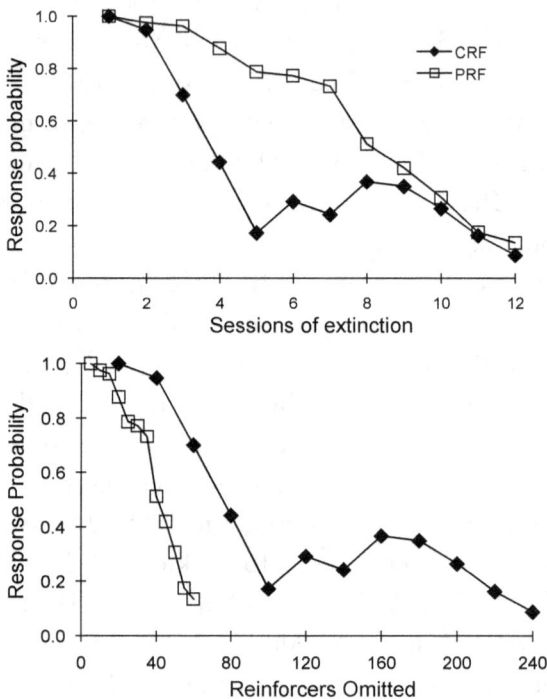

Figure 7.1. The upper panel presents the probability of pecking in discrete trials during extinction, where one or the other of two keys was lighted successively and turned off after a peck or after 5 s. For one key, reinforcers were available on every trial during training (CRF), and for the other, reinforcers were available on 25% of the trials (PRF). The result exemplifies the PREE. The lower panel replots these data with omitted reinforcers rather than sessions on the *x*-axis. From Nevin & Grace (2005).

of extinction. As shown in the upper panel of Figure 7.1, the average probability of pecking – i.e., the number of trials with a peck divided by total trials, averaged across pigeons – decreased sooner and faster on CRF than on PRF trials.

This result exemplifies the PREE in a within-subject procedure much like those employed in the research on resistance to change reviewed in Chapters 3-6; however, the finding that resistance to extinction was greater in trials with less frequent reinforcement is the exact opposite of the findings described in earlier chapters. This study, which I often described to colleagues but didn't publish until 2005, is one source of the minus (–) sign in Table 3.2 (Chapter 3).

Another contradiction came up within this simple experiment. When the birds were given food in their home cages before a session (prefeeding), or during the interval between trials (ICI food), key pecking was less disrupted on the CRF than on the PRF key, exactly opposite to extinction. As noted above, vom Saal had shown that discrete-trial stimuli signaling CRF were strongly preferred over stimuli signaling PRF, consistent with the prefeeding and ICI food results but again opposite to extinction – so there must be something unusual about extinction.

In 1988, before doing this simple experiment, I thought I had a solution to the problem posed by the PREE. Reexamining the results of a number of earlier studies, I found that if response rates during successive sessions of extinction were expressed relative to the first extinction session rather than the final sessions of baseline, the data seemed to line up with expectation – that is, responding relative to session 1 was lower and decreased more rapidly in PRF than CRF.[3] But that doesn't work for the discrete-trial data in Figure 7.1 – no matter how one transforms the response-probability data on the y-axis, PRF remains more resistant to extinction than CRF.

Another way to tackle the problem of the PREE is to rescale the x-axis to reinforcers omitted instead of time (or sessions) as in the lower panel of Figure 7.1. Randy Gallistel and John Gibbon used this method to show that extinction of autoshaped keypecking was independent of the probability of reinforcement on a trial. For example, if reinforcer probability was 1.0 during training (CRF), responding decreased to a criterion of 50% of its training level in about 45 trials, and if reinforcer probability was 0.3 (PRF), about 3 times as many trials were needed to reach the same criterion, implying that the same number of expected reinforcers – about 45 – had not occurred. Gallistel and Gibbon used these results, among others, to support their rate estimation theory, and more recently, Gallistel has invoked information theory as a formal approach to the rate estimation problem.[4]

These theoretical developments are way beyond the scope of this book; but empirically, rescaling appears to solve the problem posed for momentum theory by the data in Figure 7.1. The lower panel of that figure shows that when the x-axis is rescaled as reinforcers omitted, response probability decreases much more rapidly on PRF than on CRF trials, consistent with the notion that more frequent reinforcement generates greater resistance to change – including extinction.

The same analysis can be applied to free operant behavior. Rick Shull and Julie Grimes trained rats on single variable-interval (VI) schedules ranging from 0.25 min (240 reinforcers/hr) to 8 min (7.5 reinforcers/hr) and then conducted a single 2-hr session of extinction. They found that the number of reinforcers omitted to reach three different criteria of extinction increased systematically with the training reinforcer rate, as in the discrete-trial data in Figure 7.1. Importantly, the Shull and Grimes analysis resolves the differences between resistance to extinction after training on single *vs* multiple schedules discussed in Chapter 6.[5]

Modeling extinction

Could the momentum equations be modified to take omitted reinforcers into account? Following an approach suggested by Charlie Catania in 1973, let's ask what actually happens during extinction.[6] First, responses no longer have consequences because the operant contingency has been terminated. And second, reinforcers no longer occur, so the overall stimulus situation no longer includes food. Arguably, both of these changes are greater for the transition from CRF to extinction than for PRF. With respect to the operant contingency during training, all responses produced reinforcers on CRF, whereas some responses had no consequences on PRF. With respect to the effects of removing reinforcers considered as part of the stimulus situation, the change from the high reinforcer rate to zero, in terms of omitted reinforcers/hr, is greater for CRF than from the lower reinforcer rate to zero on PRF. If these changes are construed as disruptive forces in the momentum metaphor, it is clear that total force is greater for CRF than PRF – violating the requirement of equal forces in evaluating relative behavioral mass. So maybe CRF establishes stronger responding than PRF but extinction disrupts CRF performance more forcefully, leading to the PREE.

This purely verbal account of disruption during extinction can be expressed as a model: $x = c + dr$, where c is the disruptive effect of suspending the operant contingency, d scales the disruptive effect of removing reinforcers that occurred at rate r_s from the stimulus situation, and x represents the total disruptive force. The disruptive effect of changing the stimulus situation is known as "generalization decrement," as in studies of stimulus generalization where responding during an extinction test depends on how similar the physical stimulus (say, a red key light) is to the stimulus present during training (say, a yellow key light). The resulting "augmented" model[7] for resistance to extinction derived by adding terms to the numerator of the basic equation for resistance to change is

$$\log\left(\frac{B_t}{B_0}\right) = \frac{-t(c+dr_s)}{(r_s/r_a)^b}.$$ (7.1)

In the numerator, t represents time or successive sessions in extinction. The reinforcer rate signaled by a component stimulus, r_s, scaled by the discriminability of reinforcer omission, d, equals the generalization decrement resulting from the change in the reinforcer rate from r_s to zero; note that the product tdr_s is omitted reinforcers up to time t, scaled by d. The denominator, r_s/r_a, is the ratio of the component reinforcer rate during baseline training to the session average, r_a, which is needed to account for the finding that resistance to prefeeding and to extinction in a constant component depends inversely on the reinforcer rate in the alternated component (see Chapter 5). To get a feel for the operation of Equation 7.1, note that the disruptive force (the numerator) increases linearly with r_s, whereas behavioral mass (the denominator) increases as a power function of r_s/r_a with an

146

exponent less than 1.0 (the usual value is 0.5). Therefore, the equation predicts that resistance to extinction increases with r_s up to some point and then decreases.

Predicted extinction functions for multiple schedule components or trials with 3600 reinforcers per hr of trial time with 1-s latencies assumed (CRF) and 900/hr (PRF with p = 0.25) are shown in Figure 7.2, with $c = 0.5$, $d = 0.00001$ (upper panel) or 0.001 (lower panel). If the omission of reinforcers is relatively hard to discriminate (very small d), extinction progresses more slowly in the CRF component, but if d is relatively large, extinction progresses more slowly in the PRF component, exemplifying the PREE. Likewise, if r_s is small (as in free-operant schedules with relatively infrequent reinforcement), Equation 7.1 predicts the usual finding that responding is more resistant to change in a richer component (e.g., Figure 7.4 below), whereas if r_s is large (as in discrete trials CRF *vs.* PRF), the equation predicts the PREE (e.g., Figure 7.1 above). Importantly, the terms for behavioral mass in the denominator are unaffected by the values of c and d.

When Ant McLean came over from New Zealand to spend a semester in my lab at UNH, he suggested a way to evaluate c, the effect of suspending the operant contingency. He trained pigeons on standard multiple VI VI schedules with 60 and 15 reinforcers/hr in the components and then suspended the contingency for seven sessions by simply presenting food at the same variable times, regardless of whether the pigeons pecked – known as VT schedules (we have encountered these in Chapter 5). He found that responding decreased more rapidly in the leaner component, confirming the notion that suspending the contingency was functionally similar to prefeeding or presenting ICI

147

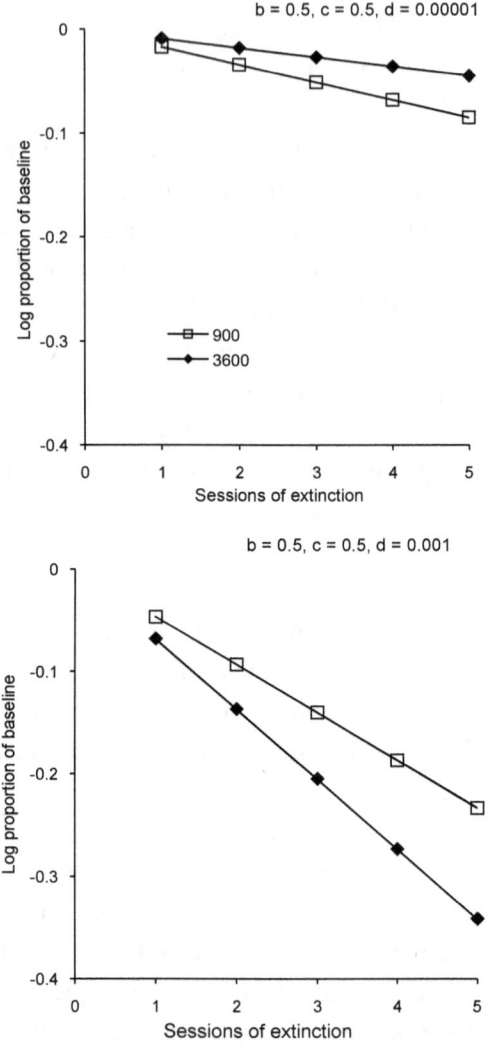

Figure 7.2. Predictions of Equation 7.1 for extinction in a multiple schedule with 3600 and 900 reinforcers/hr in the components. The upper panel shows that when the omission of reinforcers is relatively difficult to detect, extinction proceeds more rapidly in the leaner component, and the lower panel shows that when reinforcer omission is relatively easy to detect, extinction proceeds more rapidly in both components but the order of the functions is reversed, as in the data shown in the upper panel of Figure 7.1.

food, and he estimated the value of c from the data for each component. Surprisingly, it turned out to be the same for both components. Then, after reestablishing the multiple VI VI baseline, he conducted seven sessions of extinction, fitted Equation 7.1 to the data with the previously determined value of c, and obtained quite satisfactory fits with $d = 0.01$. After returning to New Zealand, Ant repeated these results with different reinforcer magnitudes, rather than different reinforcer rates, in the two components.[8]

At the same time, Randy Grace proposed a way to confirm our interpretation of d as generalization decrement – the disruptive effect of changing the stimulus situation by removing reinforcers from the components. He trained pigeons on standard multiple VI VI schedules with 120 and 30 reinforcers/hr in the components, and then conducted a single long extinction session with the component stimuli alternating as during training, but accompanied by a novel flashing light half the time. He argued that the abruptly introduced flashing light should have the same sort of effect as the abrupt discontinuation of reinforcement, and the data confirmed expectation. Taken together, Ant's and Randy's results served to validate the augmented force term in Equation 7.1 and we could apply the equation to other extinction data with some confidence.

While I was visiting New Zealand in 2000 (where Randy and Ant are on the faculty at the University of Christchurch), Randy noted that Equation 7.1 makes an interesting prediction: If extinction was arranged in the constant component only, while reinforcement continued in the alternated component, the overall context of reinforcement would change to a lesser extent – hence less disruption due to generalization decrement – than if extinction was arranged in both components. Therefore, responding in the constant component should be more resistant to extinction than when extinction was arranged in both components. The replication of my 1992 study, described briefly in Chapter 5, provided an occasion to test this prediction.

To bring the effect of changes in the alternated component reinforcer rate on the session average reinforcer rate, r_a, into the equation for extinction, we added yet another term to the numerator Equation 7.1, as shown in Equation 7.2:

$$\log\left(\frac{B_t}{B_o}\right) = \frac{-t(c + d_s r_s + d_a r_a)}{(r_s / r_a)^b} . \tag{7.2}$$

The notion is that the full disruptive effect of omitting reinforcers during extinction includes reinforcers that would have been experienced in the experimental context as well as in a component.

Figure 7.3 presents the relevant comparisons for the average weighted proportions of baseline. The left bars show that responding was more resistant to prefeeding in the constant 40/hr component when the alternated component was lean (6.67 reinforcers/hr) than when it was rich (200 reinforcers/hr); as noted in Chapter 4, the effect of the alternated component reinforcer rate was even clearer than in my 1992 study. The center bars show that resistance to extinction in the constant component was greater when the alternated schedule was lean than when it was rich, again confirming my earlier data. Finally, comparing the center and right bars shows that resistance to extinction in the constant

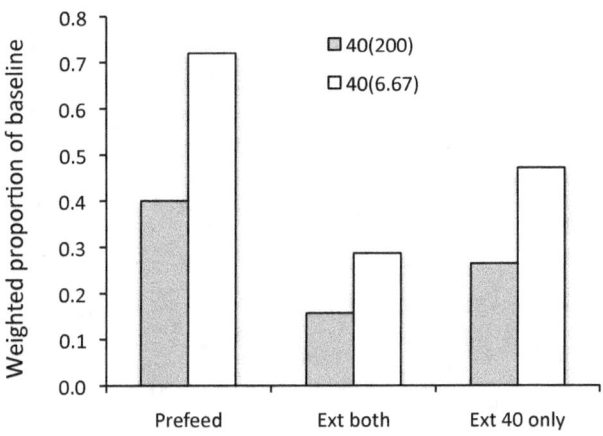

Fig. 7.3. Resistance to prefeeding and extinction, expressed as weighted proportions of baseline, in a multiple-schedule component with 40 reinforcers/hr alternated with 200/hr or 6.67/hr as indicated in parentheses. The left bars represent resistance to prefeeding, the center bars represent resistance to extinction in the 40/hr component when responding is also extinguished in the alternated component, and the right bars represent extinction in the 40/hr component when reinforcement remained available in the alternated component. Redrawn from the data of Grace et al. (2003).

component was greater when reinforcement continued in the alternated schedule than when it was discontinued in both components, representing the effect of $d\, r_a$ in the numerator of Equation 7.2. These results confirm the role of changing the context of reinforcement as a disruptor during extinction.[9]

It is only fair to ask how well Equation 7.2 performs on my 1992 data on the effects of reinforcer rate in an alternated component on resistance to change in a constant component in two-component multiple VI VI schedules (see Chapter 5; note that the extinction model had not yet been developed, so the experiment was not designed as a test). To review: In the first experiment, a constant 60 reinforcer/hr

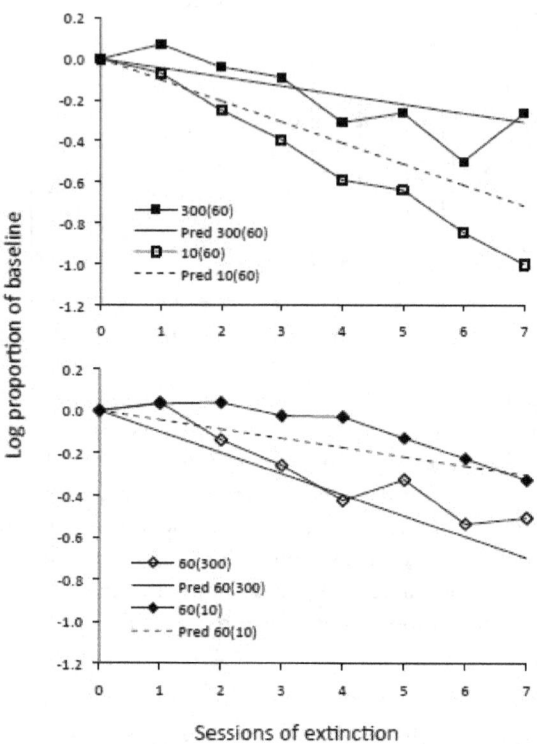

Figure 7.4. Extinction data from Nevin (1992) plotted as log proportions of baseline in 7 consecutive sessions of extinction. The lower panel presents the results for the constant VI 60/hr component alternating with either 300/hr or 10/hr [noted as 60(300) and 60(10) in the legend]. The upper panel presents the results for the alternated component in conditions with either 300/hr or 10/hr [300(60) or 10(60) in the legend]. Data are replotted from Nevin (1992), Experiment 1. The solid lines are predictions of Equation 7.2 for multiple VI 300/hr, 60/hr; the dashed lines are predictions for multiple VI 10/hr, 60/hr with parameters $b = 0.5$, $c = 0.06$, $d = 0.00005$, and $d_a = 0$.

component alternated with either 300 or 60 reinforcers/hr in successive experimental conditions, with 1-min components separated by 2-s intercomponent intervals (ICIs). Figure 7.4 presents the data for 7 consecutive extinction sessions expressed as log proportions of baseline (the right panel of Figure 5.5 presents these data as weighted proportions of baseline). The lower panel shows the data for the constant 60/hr component in both conditions, and the upper panel shows the data for the alternated component, which arranged either 300 or 10 reinforcers/hr in successive conditions. The most interesting finding was that resistance to change in the 60/hr component depended inversely on the reinforcer rate in the alternated component – a result that appears in the lower panel where the extinction function for 60/hr alternating with 300/hr lies below that with 10/hr. The data for the alternated component, in the upper panel, show that the extinction function for 300/hr lies above that for 10/hr, entirely consistent with multiple VI VI extinction data reviewed above.

By inspection, the equations account for the ordinal effects in the data, and fit really well to the extinction functions for 60(300) and 300(60). The predictions are too low for 60(10) and too high for 10(60), but all in all, Equation 7.2 provides a respectable account of the data. From a modeling perspective, the important result is that with the same parameter values for each extinction function, pretty good predictions fall out of a model not previously tested against these data.

Equation 7.1 can account for some effects of extinction in clinical applications. For example, Koegel and Rincover (1977, Experiment 2) evaluated the effects of extinction in a distinctively different setting after reinforcement (food plus praise) for simple tasks (e.g., clap hands) with children with autism. Training with CRF or short fixed-ratio schedules FR2 or FR5 was conducted in a therapy room, and extinction testing was conducted outdoors. Responding in the extinction setting decreased rapidly after CRF or FR2, but persisted for many trials after FR5, exemplifying the PREE.[10] These ordinal results are predicted by Equation 7.1 with relatively large d, as would be appropriate for the physical difference between the therapy room and outdoors. Two other children were trained with FR2 and then given noncontingent reinforcers (NCR) in the extinction setting; their responding persisted for about 5 times as many trials as for two children tested after FR2 without NCR. Again, the results are consistent with Equation 7.1 because disruption arising from the decrease in obtained reinforcers from FR2 to zero is greater than from FR2 to NCR.

The extinction model proposed here may also help us to understand the results of Jackie MacDonald and her colleagues at the New England Center for Children.[11] They arranged social reinforcers for problem behavior in four children diagnosed with autism according to CRF or VR3 schedules preceding extinction in successive conditions. Resistance to extinction was greater after CRF than after VR3 for all four children; indeed, responding increased substantially in the CRF condition, as in the rich-component data obtained by Sara Shettleworth (Figure 7.4). Although Equation 7.1 cannot account for increases in response rate during extinction, the overall difference between CRF and VR3 can be understood within its terms. MacDonald and her colleagues used short extinction sessions (5 min) in the therapy room and the person who had delivered reinforcers

154

remained in the room; therefore, disruption attributable to generalization decrement, dr_s, may have been quite small even though r_s was large.

Does extinction alter behavioral mass? Evidence from recovery

At the beginning of this chapter, I noted that because reinforcers are never delivered during extinction, behavioral mass should diminish unless the effects of training history persist throughout many sessions of nonreinforcement. The issue is related to the ancient theoretical distinction between learning and performance: Is responding unlearned during extinction, or is it merely unperformed while prior learning remains intact? And how might one find out?

In 1964, Sara Shettleworth, an undergraduate in my learning theory seminar at Swarthmore, examined pigeons' resistance to extinction in a single 5.5-hr session after extensive training on multiple VI 2-min, VI 6-min schedules. She found that after an initial increase in response rate in the richer component, extinction was substantially more rapid, relative to baseline, in the leaner component. Her data, cited in Chapter 3, were published in 1974 as Experiment 2; the average data for each component are presented in the upper panel of Figure 7.5 to illustrate their convergence as both go to zero.[12]

If extinction gradually erases the effects of reinforcement, the convergence of the component response rates makes sense because the components no longer arranged differential reinforcement that would support different behavioral masses. However, in the lower panel of Figure 7.4, where the data are expressed as log proportions

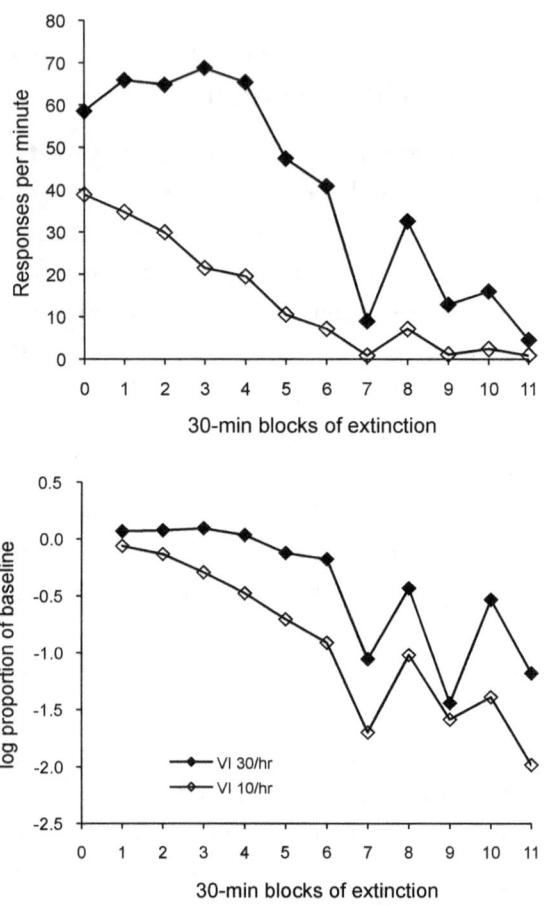

Figure 7.5. The upper panel shows response rates in the last session of training (at 0 on the *x*-axis) and during 30-min blocks of a single 5.5-hr session of extinction, averaged for 3 pigeons. The lower panel shows the data reexpressed as average log proportions of baseline. From Nevin (1974, Experiment 2).

of baseline, the standard measure of resistance to change introduced in Chapter 4, they appear to diverge in much the same way as resistance functions for ICI food where reinforcer rates are unchanged during testing for (e.g., Figure 4.1). This view of the data suggests that the elimination of reinforcers might reduce response rates but leave intact the difference in behavioral masses established by the baseline schedules. How might one decide between these interpretations?

Recovery after extinction

One possible approach is to look at post-extinction recovery of responding. If the effects of different reinforcer rates had been wiped out during extinction, recovery when reinforcers were reintroduced should be the same in both components. Not so. Figure 7.6 presents data for a group of pigeons trained on multiple VI 30s (120/hr), VI 120s (30/hr) from a laboratory class project at Utah State University, courtesy of Amy Odum and her students.[13] The figure shows that extinction responding decreased relatively more rapidly in the leaner component, confirming results described above. When responding was reinstated by presenting two response-independent reinforcers in each component – thus briefly restoring reinforcers to the stimulus situation, equally in both components – responding recovered in both components, and the difference in response rates was similar to that before extinction. Therefore, the effects of different reinforcer rates on behavioral mass evidently endured through six sessions of extinction. However, these data are not entirely conclusive because responding did not reach zero during extinction.

More persuasive data came from a series of studies in

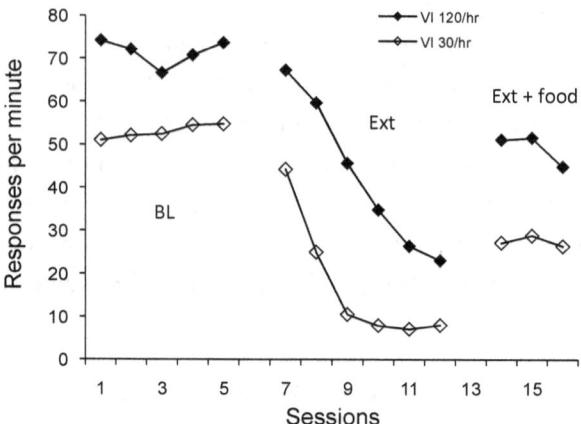

Figure 7.6. Rates of responding in a multiple VI 120/hr, VI 30/hr schedule during baseline training, extinction, and reinstatement with response-independent reinforcers; with thanks to Amy Odum and Psych 3400, Utah State University.

the USU laboratories by Chris Podlesnik and Tim Shahan.[14] They trained rats and pigeons on multiple schedules with different reinforcer rates or amounts in the components, or with added response-independent reinforcers in one component as described in Chapter 5. After baseline response rates were stable, they conducted extinction sessions until responding decreased to near zero. They then examined post-extinction recovery in three ways: Presenting a few response-independent reinforcers (as in Fig. 7.6), restoring stimulus conditions prevailing during training, where recovery is known as renewal, and removing alternative reinforcers, where recovery is termed resurgence. We will consider their studies with added VT reinforcers in one component because the usual result is that response rate is lower but resistance to change is greater in that component. Would post-extinction recovery exhibit the same ordering of response rates as

158

in baseline, or would it reflect the effects of added VT reinforcers on resistance to change?

In their renewal experiment, pigeons were trained on multiple schedules with VI 30/hr in one component and VI 30/hr with added VT 180/hr in the other component, as in several studies described in Chapter 5. The houselight was on continuously throughout training. During extinction, the houselight flashed on and off every 0.1 s, and responding decreased to near zero but relatively more slowly in the added-VT component, consistent with previous findings. Finally, the houselight was lighted continuously throughout four additional extinction sessions, and responding recovered to a substantially greater extent in the Rich, VI+VT component when the stimulus conditions that had prevailed during training were restored, suggesting that the effects of stimulus-reinforcer relations during training had persisted without reintroducing reinforcers. The results, shown in Figure 7.7, are directly relevant to a common problem with treatment for drug abuse: Even though an abuser may refrain entirely during rehabilitation in a clinic or supervised halfway house, he or she is very likely to resume drug use upon return to the environment in which abuse previously occurred.

Here's an anecdotal example. Ever since I went to college, I smoked a pipe 2 or 3 times a day. As a professor at UNH, I often loaded my pipe and went out for a stroll around the campus to plan an upcoming lecture or ponder a research problem. After retiring and moving to Martha's Vineyard, I quit smoking, cold turkey – it was pretty easy in this relatively novel environment – but then I revisited UNH. The moment I stepped onto the campus, I was overwhelmed with the desire to smoke and would surely have succumbed if pipe and tobacco had been available. Renewal!

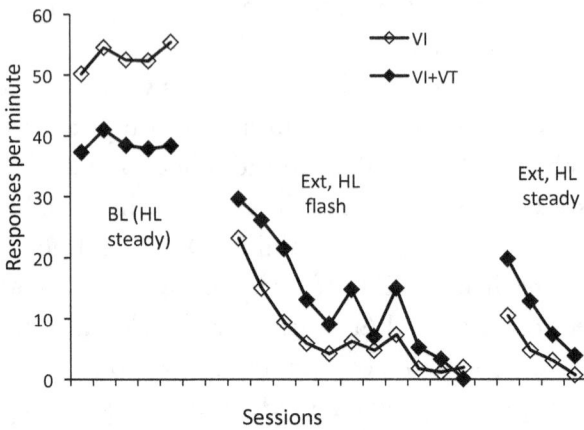

Figure 7.7. Rates of responding in a multiple VI 20/hr, (VI 20/hr+VT 100/hr) schedule in baseline with a steady houselight, extinction with a flashing houselight, and restoration of the steady houselight. Note that responding in the VI+VT component is lower during baseline but is more resistant to extinction and recovers to a higher level in subsequent experimental conditions, illustrating renewal. Redrawn from the data of Shahan & Podlesnik (2009).

Back to the lab. In a separate experiment studying resurgence, Podlesnik and Shahan arranged the same multiple VI, VI+VT schedules for pecks on a center key. Again consistent with previous findings, baseline response rate was lower in the added-VT component (see Chapter 5). During extinction, all center-key reinforcers and VT food were discontinued as in the renewal procedure, and side-key pecks were reinforced on a VI 30-s (120/hr) schedule in both components. (Note that this is a DRA schedule that combines extinction for a target response with reinforcement for an alternative response, a standard method for reducing problem behavior in clinical applications; see Chapters 5 and 9.) After center-key responding decreased to near zero,

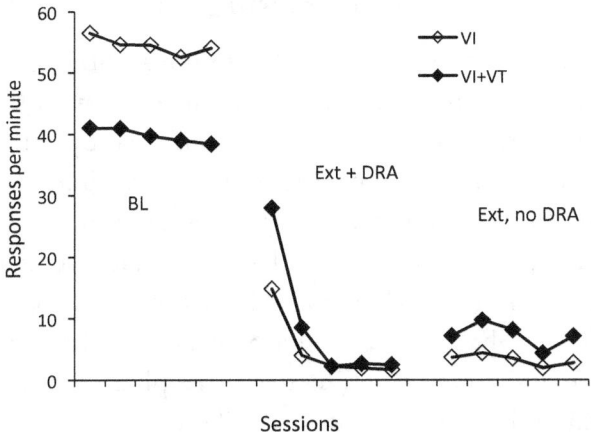

Figure 7.8. Rates of responding in a multiple VI 20/hr, (VI 20/hr+VT 100/hr) schedule in baseline, extinction with concurrent reinforcement for an alternative response, and termination of alternative reinforcement. As in Figure 7.7, responding in the VI+VT component is lower during baseline but is more resistant to extinction and recovers to a higher level in subsequent experimental conditions, illustrating resurgence. Redrawn from the data of Shahan & Podlesnik (2009).

reinforcement for side-key responding was discontinued in both components for two consecutive 5-session blocks. As shown in Figure 7.8, center-key responding increased in both components – an effect known as resurgence – but the increase was greater in the added-VT component. The implication, for clinical applications, is that if treatment with DRA is suspended for any reason, problem behavior may relapse. In their classic 1950 textbook entitled "Principles of Psychology," Fred Keller and Nat Schoenfeld used the term "regression" for this sort of outcome, and discussed it in relation to clinical problems – so the issue has been recognized for many years.

Modeling resurgence

All these data are consistent with the surprising notion that the behavioral mass of a discriminated operant that had been trained to asymptote was unaffected by extinction, supporting arguments in the literature of learning theory to the effect that extinction affects performance but does not abolish learning. To see this, we'll consider an extension of the extinction model, Equation 7.1, that was developed at USU by Tim Shahan and Maggie Sweeney for the resurgence of post-extinction responding in a three-phase procedure like that used in the example above. In Phase 1, a target response is reinforced intermittently; in Phase 2, that response undergoes extinction while, concurrently, an alternative response is reinforced; and in Phase 3, the alternative response also undergoes extinction. The model is

$$\log\left(\frac{B_t}{B_o}\right) = \frac{-t(c + dr + pr_{alt})}{((r_s + r_{alt})/r_a)^{0.5}} \, , \qquad (7.3)$$

where alternative reinforcement, r_{alt}, appears in the numerator as a disruptor with its disruptive effect scaled by p. It also appears in the denominator because alternative reinforcers are presented in the same overall situation as target reinforcers r_s.[15]

The equation predicts that in Phase 2, extinction will proceed quite rapidly because alternative reinforcement serves as an added disruptor in the numerator. When alternative reinforcers are discontinued in Phase 3, the numerator decreases, so responding must increase, and the increase will be greater if r_s was larger during baseline training, as when VT reinforcers were added to one component. As time passes, though, the value of t continues to increase so the magnitude of resurgence is predicted to decrease.

The resurgence model is directly relevant to applications where extinction of problem behavior is combined with reinforcement of desirable alternative behavior (DRA). As we have seen, a low level of responding during treatment with extinction plus alternative reinforcement does not mean that the pre-treatment history of reinforcement has been abolished. In practical terms, even a temporary lapse in providing alternative reinforcement can lead to recovery of problem behavior to a level greater than it would have been in the absence of that intervention. For example, Volkert and her colleagues observed resurgence in 3 children with autism or developmental disabilities who exhibited self-injury, aggression, or disruption. After baseline evaluation, they received functional communication training (FCT), whereby participants can obtain reinforcers by an alternative response that names the desired reinforcer (termed "manding"). After FCT performances were well established, the FCT schedule was changed abruptly from FR1 to extinction or to FR12. In every case, problem behavior increased relative to its level during extinction plus FCT, sometimes to levels well in excess of baselines before FCT was introduced.[16]

Another example has been reported by David Wacker and his colleagues. Working in the parents' homes, they arranged FCT on short ratio schedules for children with developmental disabilities who exhibited destructive and aggressive behavior. Over the course of many sessions, the FCT ratio was gradually increased from FR1 to FR8 (known as schedule thinning), and was occasionally suspended for 3-session blocks. As shown in Figure 7.8 (grey bars), problem behavior was reduced substantially relative to its initial level

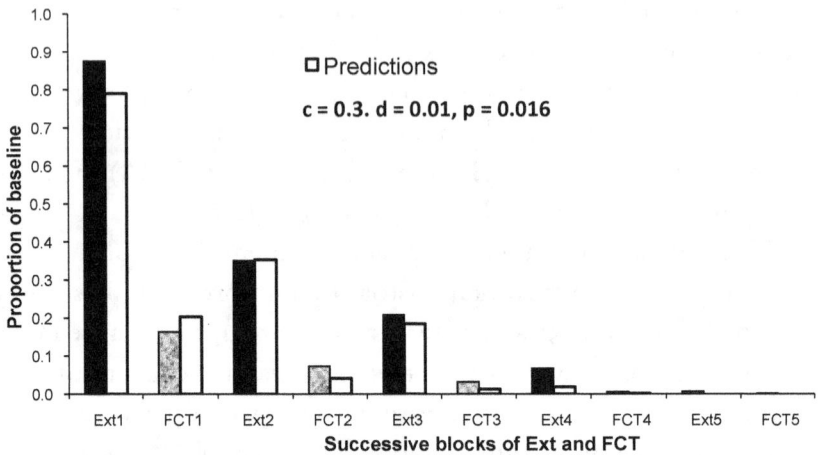

Figure 7.9. Proportions of baseline destructive behavior averaged over 7 children during successive blocks of FCT sessions in which alternative behavior was reinforced (grey bars) and interspersed extinction sessions (black bars). The predictions of Equation 7.3, with c = 0.3, d = 0.01, and p = 0.016, appear as white bars. Redrawn from the data of Wacker et al. (2012).

(Ext 1). As predicted, substantial resurgence of destructive behavior occurred in the first few extinction tests (black bars), but its magnitude decreased over successive tests, and after several months, resurgence was negligible. As shown in Figure 7.9, the average data are well described by Equation 7.3 with c = 0.3, d = 0.01, and p = 0.016.

In summary, an extension of the basic momentum equation that treats the effects of contingency termination and reinforcer omission as independent disruptors can provide an account of responding during extinction after training with a wide range of reinforcer rates. The model can account for the PREE as well as the usual finding of greater resistance to disruption in the richer of two multiple VI VI schedule components. In relation to the traditional distinction between learning and performance in behavior theory, the model implies that extinction disrupts well-established performance in the same way as other disruptors such as prefeeding or ICI food in that the value of behavioral mass based on a prior history of reinforcement (i.e. learning) is not affected. Finally, the model can be extended to account for the effects of alternative reinforcement during extinction, and for the magnitude of relapse when alternative reinforcers are discontinued. That's a long way from where I started worrying about extinction in 1988.

Chapter 8

Resistance to Change of Discriminating, Attending, and Remembering

Behavior has many more dimensions than the rate of emitting a simple response repeatedly in time. Even a pigeon's key peck may vary in its forcefulness or timing relative other responses, or the accuracy with which it is directed at one of several keys. So an obvious question is whether the same principles of behavioral momentum that hold for the sheer output of behavior (number of responses per unit time) would hold also for the quality of behavior – how accurately it conforms to the contingencies of reinforcement that define what it means to be "correct." Specifically, would the resistance to change of accuracy depend directly on reinforcer rate in the same way as the resistance to change of response rate, as illustrated in earlier chapters? A series of studies conducted jointly with Amy Odum and Tim Shahan, first at the University of New Hampshire and later in their pigeon lab at Utah State University, suggest that the answer is Yes.

166

Conditional discrimination and matching to sample

Our experiments employed the conditional discrimination paradigm, which was introduced into experimental psychology by Karl Lashley in 1938. In a simple version, the experimenter presents one of two different stimuli in successive trials, the subject can make either of two responses, and the correct response is defined by a rule – for example, if red peck left, if green peck right – and is eligible for reinforcement.

Amy and Tim and I used a version of the conditional-discrimination paradigm called matching to sample. The standard pigeon version goes like this: After an intertrial interval with all keys dark, the center key in a 3-key chamber is lighted red or green (the sample), alternating randomly over successive trials. After the bird pecks the key, the side keys are lighted, one red and the other green (the comparisons), with left and right positions switching randomly from trial to trial. The trial ends after a side key is pecked, and food is available for pecking the side key with the same color as the center key.

Variations in the procedure are easy to arrange. For example, if the sample remains lighted when the comparisons are presented, the procedure is known as simultaneous matching and accuracy is usually high; more commonly, the sample goes off when the comparisons come on. For the study of short-term memory, a retention interval is inserted between sample offset and comparison onset so the bird has to remember the sample, and accuracy decreases as the retention interval increases.

I have a certain fondness for this "delayed matching-to-sample" or DMTS procedure. When I was a graduate student at Columbia, I worked as a research assistant with

Bob Berryman and Bill Cumming on a series of DMTS experiments. One of their studies compared the accuracy of pigeons' responses to the comparisons on trials with simultaneous matching and trials with retention intervals ranging from 0 to 24 seconds, all mixed within sessions. Not surprisingly, the pigeons did best on simultaneous matching, with accuracy decreasing in an orderly way as the retention interval increased; they never did much better than chance at 24 seconds, even after 60 sessions of training.[1]

The relation between accuracy and the length of the retention interval is known as the "forgetting function." Only much later did I recognize that the forgetting function is like a resistance function, where remembering the sample, which is necessary for accurate comparison-key pecking, is challenged or disrupted by the passage of time.

Measuring accuracy of a conditional discrimination

There are different ways to measure accuracy that have implications for interpreting changes and comparing them with changes in other aspects of behavior. To make the following material clear, I will refer to the matrix of stimuli and responses displayed in Figure 8.1 that is often used to characterize conditional discriminations like matching-to-sample or signal detection.

The upper matrix illustrates red-green matching to sample, with + and − indicating correct or incorrect responses. The lower matrix provides generic notation, where (for example), S_1 and S_2 refer to the sample stimuli, such a vertical or slanted lines on the center key in Figure 8.1. B_1 and B_2 refer to responses to the comparison lines; thus, B_1 is correct on S_1 trials, and B_2 is correct on S_2 trials. B_2 on S_1 trials and B_1 on S_2 trials are errors and are never reinforced. The

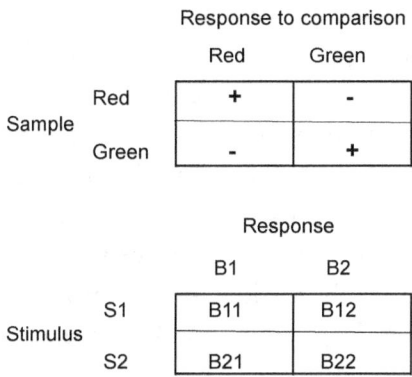

Fig. 8.1. Matrices representing stimuli, responses, and outcomes in conditional discriminations. The specific stimuli at the top are often used in matching-to-sample research with pigeons; the generic version at the bottom applies to any two-stimulus, two-response conditional discrimination.

numbers of responses recorded in each cell of the matrix are designated by row-column notation.

The overwhelming majority of research on conditional discrimination learning and performance has used proportion correct to measure accuracy, which is like a test score and makes intuitive sense. In terms of the matrix, proportion correct is equal to $(B_{11}+B_{22})/(B_{11}+B_{12}+B_{21}+B_{22})$. Proportion correct has an upper limit at 1.0, and its natural lower limit is at chance, 0.5. If proportion correct is very high – say, 0.98 – a decrease to 0.96 during disruption looks small; but in fact the number of errors has doubled, and from that perspective accuracy has changed a lot. In addition, response bias can have a major impact on proportion correct: for example, a tendency to peck the right key on most trials will lower accuracy even if the stimuli are easy to discriminate.

A good way to get around these difficulties is to express

accuracy as the logarithm of the ratio of correct responses to errors: There's no upper limit, and the lower limit – chance, when errors are exactly as frequent as correct responses – is 0. Because there are two sorts of correct responses and two sorts of errors corresponding to trials with the two different sample stimuli, we have to consider ratios separately for each sample. So throughout this chapter we will use a measure known as log d, which was introduced into behavioral analyses by Michael Davison and Donald Tustin in 1978:[2]

$$\log d = 0.5 \log \left(\frac{B_{11}}{B_{12}} * \frac{B_{22}}{B_{21}} \right), \qquad 8.1$$

which is the logarithm of the geometric mean of the ratios of correct responses to errors on S_1 and S_2 trials. Importantly, log d is like response rate in that it has no inherent upper limit and its lower limit is 0, so the effects of reinforcement and disruption on accuracy can be compared with effects on response rate. Davison and Tustin identified log d with the discriminability of the stimuli.

Davison and Tustin also suggested that response bias, log b, could be measured similarly:

$$\log b = 0.5 \log \left(\frac{B_{11}}{B_{12}} * \frac{B_{21}}{B_{22}} \right), \qquad 8.2$$

which is the logarithm of the geometric mean of the ratios of responses to alternatives 1 and 2 on S_1 and S_2 trials. If accuracy and bias are independent, log d will vary only

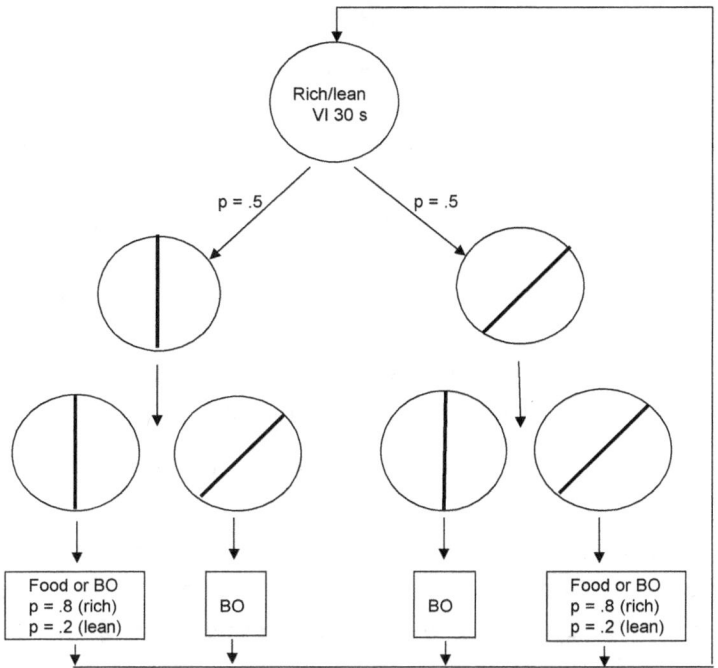

Fig. 8.2. Schematic diagram of matching-to-sample procedure with vertical and slanted lines as samples and comparisons. Probabilities of food reinforcement for correct matches were 0.8 or 0.2, signaled by the color of the center key. From Nevin et al. (2004).

with the difference between S_1 and S_2, whereas log b will vary only with the relative values of payoffs and costs. Our studies of the resistance to change of DMTS accuracy generally employed equal payoffs for the two kinds of correct responses, so there were no systematic response biases in our data and we will not pursue this aspect of performance here.

At the time when the Davison-Tustin article appeared, I was working on effects of differential reinforcement on conditional discriminations with rats where stimuli differed in brightness and responses were defined as pressing the

left or right lever in a standard rat chamber. Michael and
I started corresponding, exchanged visits between New
Hampshire and New Zealand, and spent 20 years exploring
ways to bring the fundamentals of stimulus control, choice,
and reinforcement to bear on a wide variety of conditional
discrimination results. In 1999, we published the most
comprehensive version of our modeling efforts, which will be
relevant below.[3]

Resistance to change in conditional discriminations

To explore the resistance to change of accuracy, we
needed a procedure that was analogous to multiple schedules
of reinforcement. When Amy Odum and Tim Shahan were
graduate students at West Virginia University, working with
David Schaal, they had done an interesting variation on
the DMTS paradigm. Their pigeons were required to peck
on a center key to produce DMTS trials according to a
variable-interval (VI) schedule, so that DMTS trials served as
reinforcers for VI responding, much like the terminal links
of a chain schedule. The value of the VI schedule differed
between two multiple-schedule components, so the effects of
reinforcer rate on both response rate and matching accuracy
could be evaluated within a single session – as in all the
multiple-schedule studies of resistance to change described in
earlier chapters.[4]

At UNH, we adopted the multiple VI DMTS paradigm
and arranged equal VI 30-s schedules but different
probabilities of reinforcement for correct responses: 0.8 in
the rich component and 0.2 in the lean component, signaled
by red or green key lights during the VI. We really had no
idea how various disruptors might affect accuracy, so we

used vertical and slanted lines as samples and comparisons where the slant could be chosen to establish intermediate levels of accuracy in baseline that could go up or down during disruption. The procedure, with no retention interval, is characterized in Figure 8.2. Jessie-Sue Milo, a UNH undergraduate, took the lead in running the experiment and analyzing the data.

After the pigeons achieved stable VI response rates and DMTS accuracies in both components, we disrupted performance in ways that are familiar from previous chapters – prefeeding, ICI food, and extinction. In addition, we abruptly increased the retention interval from 0 to 3 s in one condition. The average results are shown in Figure 8.3, with response rates in the upper panels and accuracy expressed as log d in the lower panels. Baseline response rates and DMTS accuracies (left panels, averaged over all baseline determinations) were higher in the rich component. During five-session blocks of disruption, both response rates and accuracies were more resistant to change in the rich component (right panels). The effects of prefeeding, ICI food, and extinction on response rate and accuracy were similar in their relative magnitude, but increasing the retention interval from 0 to 3 s had whopping effects on accuracy with much smaller effects on response rate. Despite this discrepancy in the magnitude of the disruptive effect of the retention interval, the rather satisfying overall conclusion is that accuracy of conditional discrimination, like response rate, was higher and more resistant to change in the richer of two schedule components.[5]

Delayed matching and remembering

Our next experiment extended this approach to

173

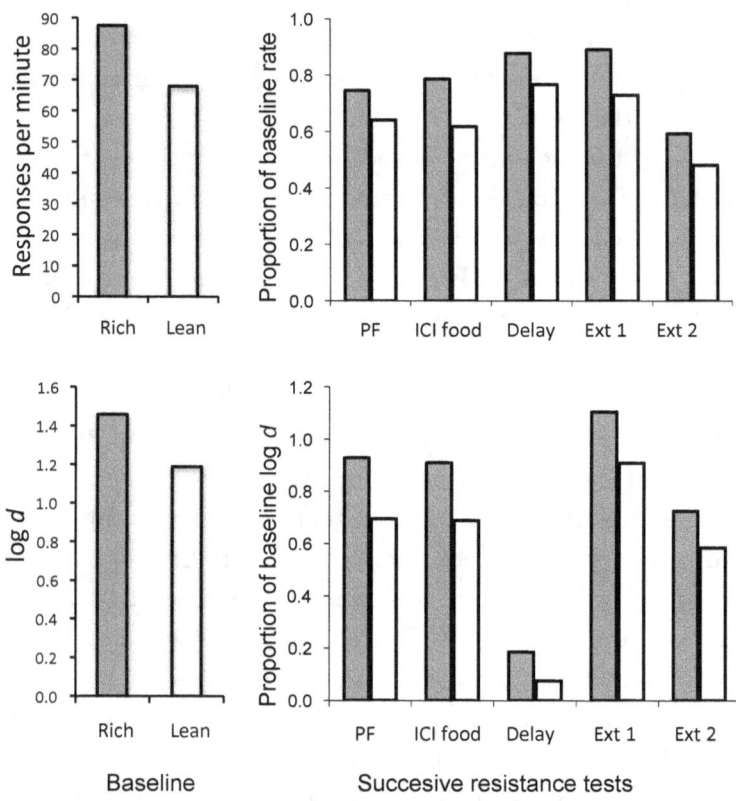

Fig. 8.3. Average data for center-key response rates (upper panels) and matching accuracies (lower panels); filled and unfilled bars show data for trials with reinforcer probabilities of 0.8 and 0.2, respectively. The left panels display baseline rates and accuracies, and the right panels display proportions of baseline during successive tests of resistance to change; Ext 1 and Ext 2 refer to successive 5-session blocks of extinction. Redrawn from data of Nevin et al. (2004).

174

forgetting functions. To compare functions within subjects and conditions, we arranged four retention intervals – 0.1, 2, 4, and 8 s – in random order within each component, and switched from lines to colors as samples and comparisons in order to get reasonably high levels of accuracy at the longer intervals. Also, we used reinforcer probabilities of 0.9 and 0.1 in the rich and lean components, rather than 0.8 and 0.2, to amplify the expected differences between components.[6]

Figure 8.4 shows that VI response rates in the rich component were higher in baseline and more resistant to disruption by ICI food and extinction, similar to the findings shown in Figure 8.3. The figure also shows average forgetting functions in baseline and during disruption, expressed as proportions of baseline log d at each retention interval. Forgetting functions were consistently higher in the rich component in baseline, as for response rates, and the slopes of the functions – the forgetting rates – were similar. During disruption by ICI food or by extinction, the overall levels of DMTS accuracy decreased less in the rich component, relative to baseline, but the effects on forgetting functions differed in subtle ways: With ICI food, the difference between components was largest at the longer retention intervals, whereas with extinction, the difference was largest at the shorter intervals. The important conclusion, though, is that forgetting functions, like response rates, were higher in baseline and more resistant to change in the rich component, confirming and extending the results of our first experiment.

The last of our major studies, conducted with USU graduate students Corina Jimenez-Gomez and Ryan Ward, attempted to separate resistance to change of forgetting functions from their baseline levels. The VI response-rate

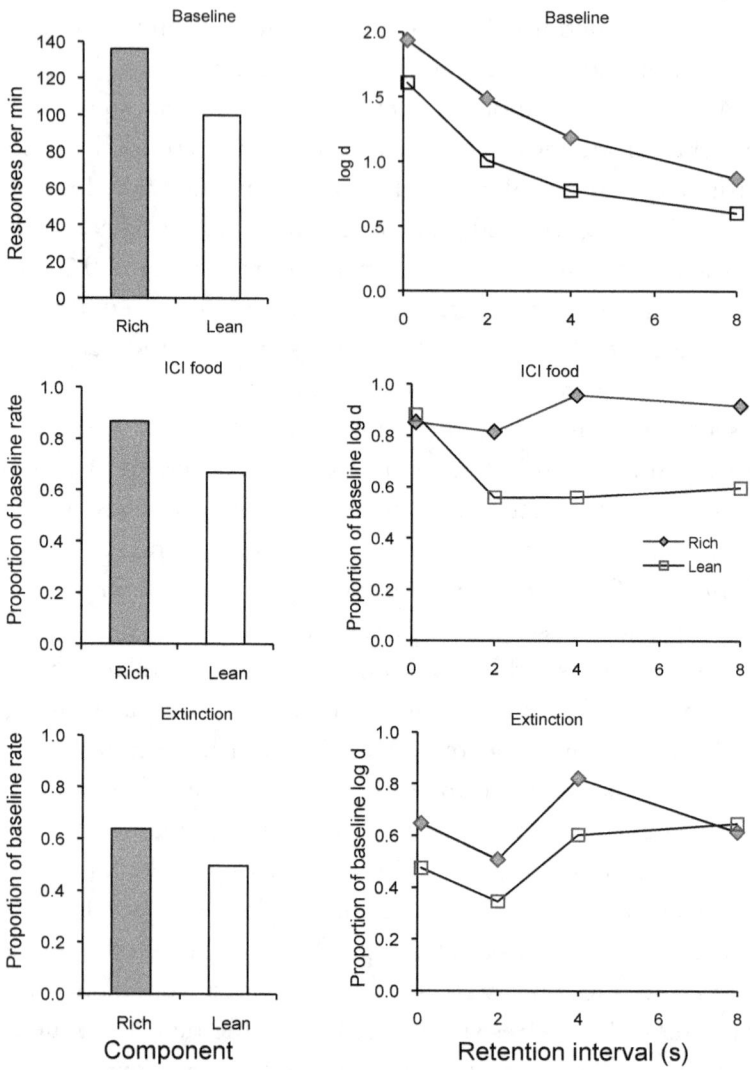

Fig 8.4. The top left panel shows baseline response rates, and the top right panel shows accuracy (log d) as functions of the retention interval (forgetting functions) in rich and lean components with reinforcer probabilities of 0.9 and 0.1, respectively. The middle panels show proportions of baseline response rate and accuracy during disruption by ICI food, and the bottom panels show proportions of baseline during extinction. Redrawn from the data of Odum et al. (2005).

data described above are functionally similar to my 1974 data (Chapter 3) in that baseline response rates and accuracies were higher and their resistance to change was greater in the richer component. Chapter 3 also described some cases in which resistance to change depended on the reinforcer rate but not on the response rate in a component. Might the same be true for DMTS accuracy?

To explore this possibility, we exploited the finding that accuracy is higher when different outcomes are arranged for the two correct side-key responses – a result known as the Differential Outcomes Effect (DOE). For example, in a 1980 study at the University of Minnesota, Peterson and colleagues trained one group of pigeons in red-green matching to sample where correct responses to green comparisons were followed by tone plus food, but correct responses to red comparisons were followed by tone only. A second group received tone plus food for all correct side-key responses. Despite the fact that the latter group obtained more frequent food, accuracy was higher for the former, especially at longer delay intervals.[7]

Accordingly, we compared differential outcomes with same outcomes in the multiple VI DMTS paradigm, with reinforcer probabilities 0.9 and 0.1 for correct responses to yellow and blue comparisons in the different-outcome (DO) component, and probabilities 0.9 and 0.9 for responses to both colors in the same-outcome (SO) component. Note that total reinforcement for correct responses is greater in the SO component, as for the separate groups in the Peterson study described above.[8]

After 50 baseline training sessions, VI response rates were a bit higher in the SO component, consistent with its greater overall reinforcer probability, but forgetting functions

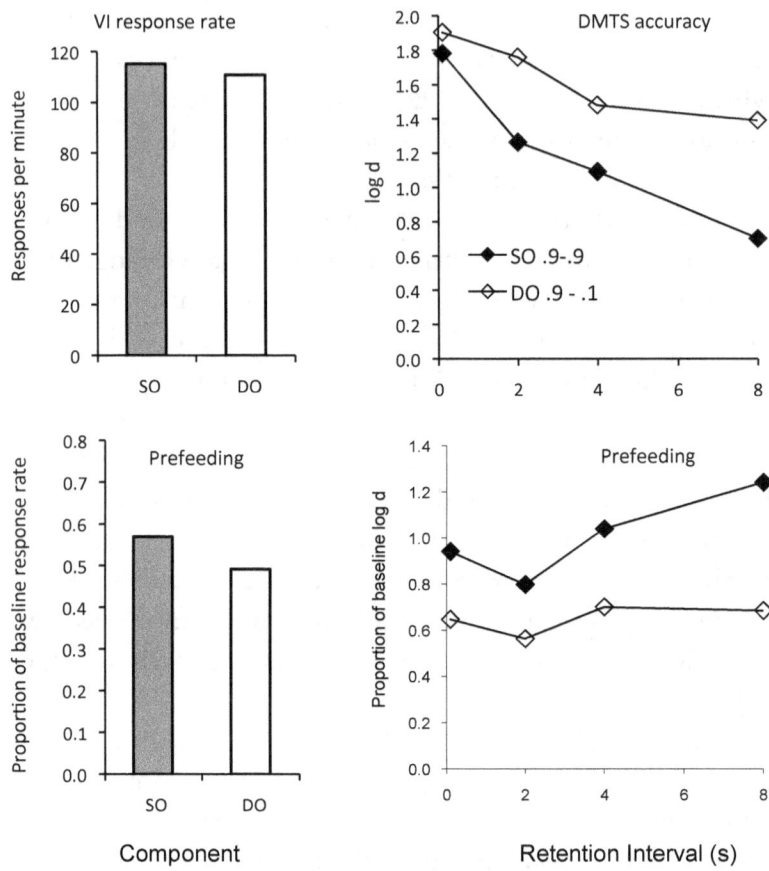

Figure 8.5. The upper left panel shows average baseline VI response rates, and the lower left panel shows the effects of prefeeding in DO and SO components, expressed as proportions of baseline response rate. The upper right panel shows average baseline matching accuracies (log *d*) as functions of the retention interval (forgetting functions). The lower right panel displays average forgetting functions during prefeeding, expressed as proportions of baseline log *d*. Redrawn from data of Nevin et al. (2009).

178

were substantially higher in the DO component for all four pigeons, replicating the standard DOE – a satisfying result for my first venture into that research area.

During disruption by prefeeding, ICI food, and extinction, all four pigeons exhibited greater decreases relative to baseline in both VI response rate and DMTS accuracy in the DO component than in the SO component. Figure 8.5 presents the results for prefeeding; strikingly, the forgetting function in the SO component remained at about 1.0 (no disruption) relative to baseline at each retention interval, whereas the forgetting function in the DO component fell to about 0.7 relative to its baseline level. Other disruptors had similar effects. Thus, the high level of DMTS accuracy maintained by differential response-reinforcer relations in the DO component was actually weaker than the lower level in the SO component – clear evidence of the dissociation of baseline accuracy and resistance to change, and a particularly powerful demonstration of the effects of reinforcer rate on resistance to change of accuracy in a multiple-schedule component.

The differential outcome effect is important outside the pigeon lab. For example, Mark Litt and Laura Schreibman taught nonverbal autistic children to choose between two objects (comparisons) after hearing their spoken names (samples), and found that the children learned the task much more rapidly when they received different but equally desirable food reinforcers for correct choices than when the same highly preferred food followed all correct responses. It would be worth pursuing this result to see if name-object relations were better remembered in the different-food or same-but-preferred food conditions.[9]

Selective attention

The studies described above have involved samples and comparisons from a single stimulus dimension such as color or line orientation. But stimuli that signal significant events in everyday life are often multi-dimensional, involving both visual and auditory stimuli such as the looming headlights and crunching gravel sound of an approaching car while you are out walking at night on a country road. When you have two cues in a compound like that, it's easy to avoid the car.

To be sure of clear differentiation between multiple-schedule components, the Shahan-Burke study described in Chapter 1 employed compounds of lights and tones, without evaluating which dimension the rats attended to because it really didn't matter. But selective attention can be problematic. A popular example (thanks to the internet) is known as "The Invisible Gorilla," where people were instructed to count basketball passes by players with white shirts in a video clip.[10] Strikingly, many of the viewers did not report seeing a person clad in a gorilla suit who had walked through the scene. Evidently, instructions blocked attending to anything but the players' shirts and actions.

Concentrating on a single aspect of a stimulus situation without noticing other elements is known as stimulus overselectivity, and it can hinder learning about relevant features of the environment, especially in people with intellectual or developmental disabilities (IDD). Bill Dube and Bill McIlvane studied stimulus overselectivity in three individuals with moderate to severe IDD, in a matching-to-sample procedure with arbitrary figures presented on a computer touch screen. During training, the samples were single figures; touching the comparison that matched the sample was reinforced according to different schedules depending on the sample. For example, matching an inverted golf tee was reinforced on 3 out of every 4 trials, whereas matching a vertical dumbbell was reinforced on 1 out of 4 trials. In test trials, the samples were compounds of two figures, and the comparisons were single figures; the question was whether the subjects would touch the comparison associated with the higher frequency of reinforcement during training.[11]

Over the course of a series of schedule changes and reversals, the answer was clearly Yes: Attention to an element of a compound depended on the frequency of reinforcement experienced with that element. Perhaps if subjects in the invisible-gorilla demonstration had a history of reinforcement for reporting nonhuman interlopers in basketball games, they would have failed to notice the shirt colors of the players.

The Dube-McIlvane study was repeated by Tim Shahan and Chris Podlesnik with pigeons using compound samples with red or green backgrounds and superimposed white vertical or horizontal lines on the center key in the pigeon chamber. To evaluate attending to color or line, comparison stimuli on left and right keys were red or green on color-only trials, and vertical or horizontal white lines on dark keys in line-only trials. The ratios of reinforcers for correct matches on color-only to line-only trials varied from 9:1 to 1:9. Accuracy on a given trial type increased as reinforcement for that type became more probable, and decreased as reinforcement became less probable, confirming the results for children with IDD.[12]

In more quantitative terms, the difference between color-trial and line-trial accuracies, expressed as log d, was a power function of the ratio of their reinforcer probabilities similar to the generalized matching law for response rates to concurrently available VI schedules (Chapter 3, Equation 3.3). Thus, choice between attending to lines versus colors, presented together in the compound samples, depended on relative reinforcer rates arranged for the elements in the same way as response rates in free-operant choice procedures.

The next question was whether the resistance to change of selective attending would conform to predictions of behavioral momentum theory. Together with Eric Thrailkill, Chris and Tim repeated that study in a multiple schedule where correct responses to color or line elements were reinforced five times more often in a rich component than a lean component. When performances were disrupted by prefeeding or by extinction, accuracy on both trial types was less disrupted in the richer component. These findings confirm and extend those described above by showing that the persistence of selective attending to an element of a compound sample is directly related to the probability of reinforcement.[13]

The momentum of attending and remembering

The finding that accuracy is functionally similar to response rate, in that resistance to change depends on reinforcer rate for both measures, raises an interesting question for the momentum metaphor. The change in response rate is at least roughly analogous to a change in the velocity of a moving body, but the same is not true for a change in accuracy.

One way to rescue the metaphor is to suggest that measured accuracy depends on the private behavior of attending and remembering, which may have rate-like

182

aspects in terms of their probability of occurrence over time. Together with Michael Davison, Amy and Tim and I devised a theoretical model which assumes that the private activities of attending and remembering during a DMTS trial are similar to the public behavior of key pecking in terms of their probability and persistence. Specifically, we derived momentum-based equations for the probabilities of attending to the sample and, separately, to the comparison stimuli, both during their actual presentation and during the retention interval when a subject must do something – called "rehearsal" – to retain information about the value of the sample.

To get a feel for our approach, consider my making a phone call on a landline in my home. I go to a directory on the kitchen counter and look up the number (i.e., attend to it) – that's the sample – and then I mutter it covertly (rehearse it) while moving toward the phone. At the phone, I have to attend to both the silently muttered rehearsal and to the number pad while dialing (the comparison response), or I will misdial even if I recall the number perfectly. These components of my behavior can be disrupted at any point – for example, if someone knocks on the door while I am moving between the directory and the phone, or if I am asked to look up another number while I am in the midst of dialing.

Developing this approach into a theoretical model required a number of assumptions, and the equations themselves are loaded with free parameters analogous to c and d in Equation 7.1 for resistance to extinction (Chapter 7). I won't go into the model here – interested readers should check out the published article – but will simply note that the model accounts for the accuracy and resistance to change of DMTS performance under several different conditions quite satisfactorily, including the examples presented in Figures 8.3 and 8.4 (although it does not predict the baseline DOE, which remains a theoretical challenge).[14]

Interestingly, the model predicts that the resistance to change of accuracy will differ between the multiple-schedule procedure described here and a closely related procedure where different reinforcer probabilities or amounts are signaled within each trial[15] rather than by component key colors that are present throughout a series of trials. To test this rather esoteric prediction, Amy, Tim, Ryan Ward, and I did the required comparison between groups of pigeons trained separately on these procedures; and to our astonishment, the prediction was confirmed! So it is fair to conclude that the momentum-based model of attending and remembering might actually be correct, at least until challenged by some new findings.[16]

In the overall scale of human affairs, or even in the smaller domain of behavioral science, this improbable confirmation of momentum-based theory is trivial. But the program of theory and research that led up to it is important because it implies that the basic ideas of momentum theory can be extended via quantitative modeling into the domain of private activities that cannot be observed directly, and can only be inferred from a set of theoretical assumptions.

The invocation of unmeasured cognitive processes such as attending, rehearsing, and remembering is anathema to most behaviorally oriented psychologists, and several of my behaviorist friends advised me to stay out of this murky domain. In fact, though, it is a direct extension and, indeed, confirmation of B. F. Skinner's radical behaviorism, which assumes that activities taking place within the skin are natural events that are functionally similar to overt action even though they cannot be measured directly.[17] In this chapter, I have treated private events indirectly by making them essential components of a momentum-based model of behavior. The success of this endeavor with pigeon performance on DMTS tasks suggests that private behavior in general, including parts of everyday human activities such as thinking about future events and anticipating outcomes, may also be subject to at least a conceptual analysis within the overall framework of behavioral momentum theory.

Chapter 9

Extensions to Clinical and Applied Settings

The broad domain known as applied behavior analysis, behavior modification, or behavior therapy is concerned with – well, *fixing* problem behavior, and only secondarily with identifying its presumed underlying causes such as developmental deficiencies or genetic factors. There's no denying the importance of those biological conditions, but there's not much one can do to alter them in the present for a given individual. Instead, let's see what we can do to help a developmentally disabled person to live as good a life as is humanly possible. That means replacing self-injurious or destructive or antisocial behavior, however well entrenched, with healthful and socially desirable behavior – and moreover, to make the newly acquired, desirable behavior as persistent as possible, so that the person will not require constant therapy in order to get along in everyday life.

Clearly, behavioral momentum theory and research are relevant to these goals. First, the old problem behavior, almost by definition, occurs frequently and is difficult to disrupt or prevent – that is, it has high momentum, presumably based at least in part on a long but poorly understood history of reinforcement. Almost certainly, a behaviorally based intervention, perhaps in concert with therapeutic drugs, will be required to disrupt it. Second, as undesirable behavior wanes, new and desirable behavior can be established – and it should be endowed with high momentum so that it occurs reliably on appropriate occasions and persists long after clinical intervention has done its job.

Before continuing, I have to issue a disclaimer: I have no direct experience in applied or clinical settings, I have never treated a client (indeed, I am not licensed to do so), and except for a couple of weeks tutoring a special-needs boy in arithmetic, I have no experience with kids with intellectual or developmental disabilities. Nevertheless, let's get more concrete about applying the momentum metaphor to clinical or therapeutic problems by considering a hypothetical first-grade boy with intellectual and developmental disabilities in a special-education program, "mainstreamed" into a regular classroom. The boy talks to himself out loud, moves about constantly, hits other kids, and ignores the teacher's instructions to sit quietly and work on class material such as drawing shapes or stacking blocks. The boy's behavior is disruptive for the other kids and prevents the teacher from working effectively with the rest of the class. How might a school psychologist or teacher eliminate, or at least reduce, this disruptive behavior? Also, how to establish new, desirable behavior, and then make it as persistent as possible so that it can compete effectively with the problem behavior in the long term?

Establishing compliance with requests

To start the process, it is necessary to evoke desirable behavior that does not, at present, exist – in our example, that would be compliance with the teacher's request to attend to classroom tasks in a quiet, nondisruptive way.

In the Introduction, I alluded to work by Bud Mace and his associates and students that brought the metaphor of momentum out of the pigeon lab and into the world of behavioral applications. In 1988, Bud described a procedure for establishing compliance with requests that were ordinarily ineffective with adults with intellectual and developmental disabilities (IDD) living in a group home, such as "Please take out the garbage" – the sorts of things that most parents of adolescent kids have to deal with every day, and that are essential components of group-home life. These sorts of requests were called "low-p" because the probability of compliance was usually well below 0.5. Mace and his associates found that if they preceded low-p requests with three "high-p" requests such as "Shake my hand," "Show me your radio," or "Give me five," each of which was easy and enjoyable and entailed some social reinforcement, the residents were much more likely to comply with a low-p request.[1]

Bud and colleagues developed this so-called "high-p" procedure without specific reference to momentum research, but the term "behavioral momentum" appeared in their title, and if you Google "behavioral momentum," you are likely to come up with the "high-p" procedure. The procedure is very different from multiple schedules with intermittent reinforcement, where various disruptors are presented after many hours of training. However, there are some metaphorical similarities in that once behavior in the response class "compliance" has been initiated and reinforced, it is more likely to persist in the face of a challenging request. And there may be some functional similarities as well. For example, the time between high-p requests must be fairly

188

short, suggesting that rate of reinforcement for compliance, such as approval, is important. Moreover, if tangible reinforcers such as food are given for complying with high-p requests, compliance is more likely to persist over several successive low-p requests.

Other researchers have found that low-p compliance can be enhanced by telling amusing stories rather than giving high-p requests, and that the method may not always work unless coupled with extinction of competing behavior. Importantly, though, the procedure has been effective in a variety of settings. For example, Carol Davis and her associates have used the procedure to establish social play in children with autism, and found that various social interactions persisted even after the procedure was discontinued. Ducharme and Worling adapted the high-p procedure for use by the parents of children with IDD to establish compliance with various low-p requests in the home, and found that low-p compliance persisted for at least 16 weeks after the number and frequency of high-p requests were gradually reduced to zero. Most relevant here, David Lee and his associates have used the high-p procedure to increase letter- and word-writing and arithmetic problem solution by special-education students who had trouble completing assigned work (and were sometimes disruptive in the classroom), so the high-p procedure might be useful for the special-ed student in my example above.[2]

To employ the high-p procedure with our hypothetical student, we would start by identifying some activities that he seems to enjoy and does without hesitation when asked – something like "Show me your baseball cards" if the boy is a sports enthusiast – and then reinforce with social approval (ideally, including attention and approval by the other kids in the class). After the boy complies with three or four such requests, the teacher could up the ante: For example, "Please finish the drawing you are working on." If the boy complies, more attention and approval follow at once. On the basis of the studies cited above, this general procedure, iterated many times, should be effective in getting the child to engage in schoolwork when asked.

The thoughtful reader will recall earlier chapters and say: "This may get some desirable behavior going but at the same time, those social reinforcers – attention and approval – are given in the classroom, so they should make disruptive behavior in that stimulus situation – the classroom – more persistent. If the teacher is distracted by other students and the child's classroom work goes unreinforced, loud talking, moving about, and hitting other kids should recur (resurgence) and actually be harder to eliminate than if the high-p procedure and its reinforcers had never been implemented." The reader is correct, and the problem is not hypothetical, as we saw in Chapters 5 and 7.

Separating reinforcers for problem and alternative behavior

In 2010, Bud Mace proposed a potential solution. Recall the 1990 study by Tota, Torquato, Shull, and myself where pigeons obtained food for pecking the right-hand key in a two-key chamber – let's take that as analog problem behavior – in three multiple-schedule components (see Chapter 5). In the DRA component, food was also available for pecking the left-hand key (analog desirable behavior), whereas the second component did not arrange an alternative source of food. The result, which bears repeating here, was that the rate of right-key pecking was lower but more resistant to change in the DRA component. (For present purposes we will ignore the third component, which provided food at a rate equal to the sum of food obtained on the left and right keys in the DRA component.)

Bud's idea was to reinforce desirable alternative behavior (hereafter BA) in a separate stimulus situation so its strengthening effects would not add to those already maintaining the target problem behavior (BT). He began by testing the idea with rats. Figure 9.1 shows the arranged rates of food reinforcers in a DRA component with concurrent reinforcement for BT (right lever) and BA (left lever), a second component with only BT available, and a third component with only BA available. Because BA was reinforced in a separate stimulus situation, where the target response was not available, the strengthening effect of alternative reinforcers on target behavior might be reduced – or even eliminated – without losing the chance to reinforce desirable alternative behavior.[3]

After extensive training on the components shown above the line in Figure 9.1, food reinforcement was discontinued, and the stimuli that had signaled reinforcement for BT-only and BA-only were presented together as a novel compound, alternating with the DRA and BT-only components. Target responding was more resistant to extinction in the DRA component than in the BT-only component, replicating the earlier results; but importantly, resistance to extinction was about the same in the component with BT only and in the novel compound with both BT and BA available. Thus, an alternative response could be reinforced in a separate component without increasing the resistance to change of the target response.

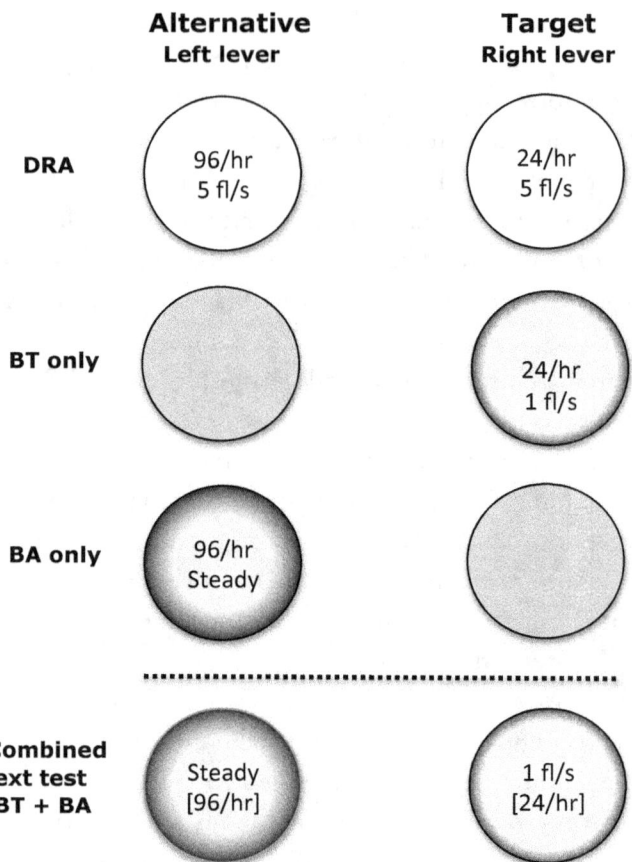

Figure. 9.1. Diagram of multiple-schedule components arranged for rats by Mace et al. (2010). The three components above the dotted line were presented in irregular alternation during training, signaled by steady or flashing lights. During subsequent extinction, these components alternated with a novel compound depicted below the line, which combines component stimuli that had separately signaled reinforcement for analog problem behavior BT and alternative behavior BA (reinforcer rates in brackets). Adapted from Mace et al. (2010).

Bud and his colleagues repeated the procedure with two human participants who exhibited severe disruptive behavior, such as shouting, throwing objects, and slapping therapists. The equivalent of the DRA, BT-only, and BA-only components were administered by therapists wearing different colored hospital gowns; thus, therapists who administered reinforcers for BT-only and for BA-only could get together to form a novel test compound. During extinction, disruptive target behavior increased in the DRA component but remained low or decreased somewhat in the BT-only component and the novel two-therapist compound, repeating the results with rats at least ordinally.

Chris Podlesnik, who got involved in research on resistance to change as a graduate student with Tim Shahan at USU (see Chapter 7) and then moved to New Zealand, has replicated Mace's work with pigeons as subjects, and removed a possible confound: Because the stimulus signaling reinforcement for BT-only was presented by itself as well as in the novel compound, it appeared twice as often as the stimuli signaling the DRA component, and target responding BT might therefore extinguish more rapidly. Working with colleagues at the University of Auckland, Chris found that resistance to extinction of BT in the novel compound after baseline training without the BT-only component was greater than when the BT-only component had also been presented, but still was less than in the DRA component. (See Figure 9.2.) The major finding is that resistance to extinction of BT was greater in the DRA component than in the novel compound, confirming Mace's results with rats and humans.

When extinction ended and a few free food presentations were given – a procedure known as reinstatement (see Chapter 7) – Chris found that responding increased substan-

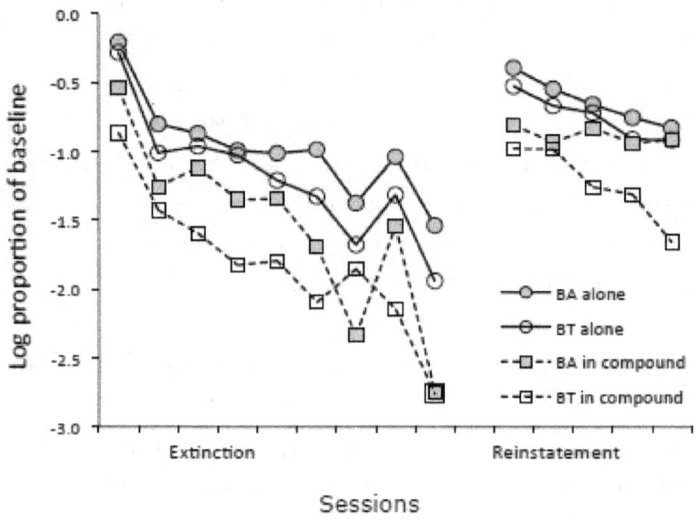

Figure. 9.2. Log proportion of baseline response rates of pigeons trained with a version of Mace's paradigm (see Fig. 9.1) during 9 sessions of extinction followed by 5 sessions of reinstatement with occasional presentations of free food. Filled and unfilled circles show data for BT and BA from the DRA component; filled and unfilled squares show data from the novel compound of signals for BT only and BA only. Note that the extinction curves for the novel compound are lower and somewhat steeper than for the DRA component, indicating that the strengthening effects of alternative reinforcement on resistance to extinction could be reduced by reinforcing alternative behavior in a different stimulus context. Note also that there was substantial relapse in all components during reinstatement. Thanks to C. Podlesnik for providing response-rate data from Podlesnik et al. (2012).

194

tially in all components. Thus, the procedure did not protect analog problem behavior, BT, from relapse.[4]

The conclusion, then, is that reinforcing alternative behavior in a different stimulus situation can reduce its strengthening effects on target behavior. However, this method may not be practical for repeated treatment because the novel combination will no longer be novel, and worse, is perfectly predictive of extinction.

As I write, a reliable, practical way to establish persistent desirable behavior by providing alternative reinforcers without also strengthening undesirable target behavior and making it prone to relapse remains to be achieved. But we're working on it. A group of researchers – Bill Ahearn at the New England Center for Children, Bill Dube at the Shriver Center, Willie DeLeon at the Kennedy Krieger Institute, Bud Mace at Nova University, and Tim Shahan at USU – are currently collaborating with me to address the problem. With support from the National Institute of Child Health and Human Development (for which thanks), we are trying to address disruptive, aggressive, or self-injurious behavior in children with various intellectual and developmental disabilities by adapting a procedure that has been used successfully to treat drug abuse.

The contingency management paradigm

A direct behavioral approach to treating drug abuse and addiction has been termed "abstinence reinforcement" or, more generally, contingency management. The basic idea is to give abusers access to a workplace that provides a safe environment where they can earn vouchers by doing various tasks and learning some useful job skills; the vouchers are

195

redeemable for food, housing, and other nondrug necessities. But to gain access to that workplace, abusing clients must provide clean urine samples demonstrating abstinence from the drug in question. Thus, abstinence is reinforced by vouchers in a situation quite different from an addict's everyday street environment.

Unlike most behavioral treatments, the target behavior of drug abuse, BT, does not undergo extinction in the addict's normal street environment (indeed, that environment is beyond experimental control, to say the least), and there is no attempt to establish desirable alternative behavior, BA, in that environment; instead, the addict must refrain from drug use in order to obtain nondrug reinforcers in a distinctly different environment. Steve Higgins and Ken Silverman are among the leaders in developing this approach, and so far have achieved considerable success.

As an example, Silverman and colleagues arranged workplace access and redeemable vouchers for opiate and cocaine abusers, and examined the proportion of clean samples obtained over 12 days before and after workplace access was made contingent on abstinence. Overall, the proportion of participants who submitted clean samples increased from about 20% to over 40% when access was contingent. A related study by Higgins and colleagues found a similar difference between groups that differed in whether vouchers were contingent upon or independent of cocaine-free urine samples. Thus, access to a workplace and vouchers can reinforce abstinence. Higgins went on to evaluate abstinence for a year after the program ended – in effect, testing resistance to extinction – and found that although abstinence decreased similarly for both groups, it remained higher for the contingent-access group.[5]

The contingency-management paradigm resembles a serial schedule: Abstinence precedes access to vouchers in the workplace. Recall, from Chapter 5, that for pigeons at least, resistance to change in the first segment of a serial schedule depends directly on the reinforcer rate in the second segment; therefore, vouchers obtained in the workplace should increase the persistence of abstinence on the street. Moreover, in serial schedules, resistance to change is pretty much the same for contingent and noncontingent access to the second segment; Higgins's data on the post-treatment persistence of abstinence, showing similar decreases for contingent and noncontingent access groups, accord with the serial-schedule findings.

A pigeon model and possible application

Encouraged by the similarities of pigeon persistence and human abstinence data, Tim Shahan, Maggie Sweeney, Andy Craig, and I are exploring a version of the contingency management paradigm with pigeons at USU; the work is part of the collaborative endeavor I mentioned above. The procedure involves three phases that are standard in modeling treatment and post-treatment relapse. First, the pigeon gets food according to a variable-interval (VI) 30/hr schedule for pecking the left key (that's analog BT) in two identical multiple-schedule components to establish equal pretreatment baselines. Then, in the "treatment" component, pecks no longer produce food, but when the pigeon abstains from pecking for 15 seconds (a DRO contingency), the right-hand key lights up with a different color (representing the workplace) and pecks at that key (analog BA) are reinforced on a VI 120/hr schedule. The other component is a no-treatment control. Finally, food reinforcers are discontinued in both components and in the "workplace." In our first efforts with this procedure, key pecking in the DRO abstinence component decreased rapidly during treatment, did not exhibit resurgence when treatment ended, and did not exhibit reinstatement in a subsequent test with response-independent food. It is as if refraining from key pecking had been strengthened by the DRO-contingent access to a richer schedule of reinforcement on the right, alternative key – an encouraging outcome.

The paradigm might be worth trying with the hypothetical first-grade boy who introduced this chapter. Suppose that his disruptive behavior could be ignored in the regular classroom until (say) a minute went by with no disruption. Then, a teacher's aide could escort the boy to an adjacent room where he could indulge in some preferred activities, and also get frequent social reinforcement from the aide for working on class material – perhaps initiated by using the high-p procedure described above. That separate room is, of course, the analog to the workplace, where alternatives to disruptive behavior can be reinforced without increasing the persistence of disruptive behavior in the regular classroom – perhaps.

There is a lot more to do with the pigeons before we can apply this paradigm to the treatment of problem behavior in children with real confidence. To be sure that the DRO contingency actually made a difference, we will have to repeat the experiment with no contingency on access to the workplace, as in the studies with drug abusers cited above. Also, it will be important to compare discontinuing food for alternative behavior in the workplace with discontinuing access to the workplace altogether. Obviously, it will be essential to ascertain whether the results generalize to kids with different sorts of problem behavior in clinical settings.

And then there's the question of how to interpret the results in relation to the momentum metaphor and the algebraic models of extinction and relapse that I described in Chapter 7. There will be no shortage of questions, challenges, and data to maintain my momentum-related activities for many years.

Postscript

At the beginning of our 1983 paper introducing the notion of behavioral momentum, Charlotte Mandell, Jean Atak, and I referred to an 1898 physics text by S. W. Holman, in which the author restated Newton's first law of motion as "All observed changes in the state of motion of bodies are due to discoverable external action."[1] We went on to propose a behavioral equivalent: "All observed changes in behavior are due to discoverable external variables."

Some of the UNH students who read the paper got upset because our statement leaves no room for the inner forces of imagination, creativity, play, or sheer cussedness to change one's behavior – or even generate altogether novel behavior. And it seems entirely incompatible with the private experience of free will, which I share with pretty much everyone I know. Many behavioral scientists have wrestled with these issues; I especially like the work of Allen Neuringer, who has related the concept of voluntary behavior to learned variability (rather the opposite of learned persistence or momentum) and Richard Rakos, who has pointed out the social and personal utility of belief in free will.[2]

Without any question, behavioral momentum theory exemplifies a mechanistic worldview. In the 1980s, I commented on some similarities between the science of evolution and the science of behavior in a symposium at the Cambridge Center for Behavioral Studies, and in a followup book chapter[3] I wrote "At the end of *The Origin of Species,* Darwin invites the reader to contemplate a tangled bank, with its plants and birds, its insects and worms; to marvel at the complexity, diversity, and interdependence of its inhabitants; and to feel awe at the fact that all of it follows from the laws of reproduction, competition, and natural selection. Our delight in the tangled bank and our love for its inhabitants are not diminished by our knowledge of the laws of evolution; neither are our delight in the complex world of activity and our love for its actors diminished by our tentative but growing knowledge of the laws of behavior." I don't think I can say it better.

Among the most fundamental principles of behavior are, first, selection of responses by reinforcement; second, choice among those responses in proportion to the reinforcers they obtain; and third, the momentum of on-going responses in the presence of stimuli that signal reinforcers. Paradoxically, these principles, which underly so much activity that can fill our lives with delight, also account for the human behavior that now threatens so many other species and contributes to the warming of the planet that supports all life.

The changing world

In the late 1950s, while I was in the Coast Guard, I spent a year as CO of a loran station on the northwest coast of Greenland. Our crew of 16, mostly technicians and support folks, was basically isolated for 12 months. We were not far from a huge glacier, and its face glistened blue and green in crystal-clear sunlight. We could hear long, rumbling sounds

201

of thunder as icebergs calved into Smith Sound, where they remained frozen into the sea ice as it moved slowly south. I fell in love with the land and its vastness and timelessness.

But now the glaciers and sea ice are melting, and I weep to see the photographs that inform us of the damage to the arctic being caused by global warming. Because global warming and related planet-wide changes are the result, in large part, of human economic activity, the problem is, in large part, behavioral. And I contribute to the activity that comprises the global economy.

Of course I know that burning fossil fuel creates CO_2, a greenhouse gas, and that my car – which I drive about 6000 miles a year, at 30+ miles/gallon – makes an annual contribution of 2 tons of CO_2 to the atmosphere. But I continue to drive almost daily, and as a result am able to enjoy a host of activities that would otherwise be difficult to engage in: going to movies and concerts, seeing friends, shopping for groceries, taking leaves to the dump – the normal round of everyday life. Thus, driving provides access to reinforcers, much more quickly and with less effort than waiting for the local bus or walking a few miles, although the latter might put a small dent in my carbon footprint.

We know, from Chapter 5, that reinforcers need not be contingent on the response of interest in order to make it more resistant to change. I am lucky to live on a beautiful island, and my house gets electricity, phone and cable service, and clean drinking water – none of which are contingent on driving. It's a comfortable life, and these comforts may well make a specific activity like driving even more resistant to change than the reinforcers that driving can provide. In terms of the momentum metaphor, my driving has a lot of behavioral mass, and is not likely to be disrupted by the latest reports that sea levels are rising much more rapidly than predicted a year or two ago, or even by big increases in the price of gasoline.[4]

Now take this argument to the level of the global economy – the vast array of activities that provide food and consumer goods from all over the world – nearly all of which depend on energy provided by fossil fuels. And the business of extracting, transporting, refining, and selling fossil fuel products provides jobs for workers, profits for shareholders, and astounding wealth for top executives. I suggest that the positively reinforcing consequences of all these activities and the relatively affluent society in which they take place have established an aggregate behavioral mass, summed over the millions who benefit from them, that makes the global fossil fuel economy extraordinarily resistant to change.

In one of my favorite articles, Skinner[5] pointed out that that the evolution of species depends on selection by consequences for successful behavioral adaptation to changing circumstances, and here I have argued that successful – that is, generously reinforced – adaptations may persist with little change in the face of challenges. It is truly tragic that these processes may now have converged to produce the slow-motion behavioral equivalent of Chicxulub, the asteroid that smashed into the Yucatan at the end of the Cretaceous period about 66 million years ago.[6] In a very short time by geological standards, the aftermath of Chicxulub wiped out the dinosaurs and countless other creatures, allowing mammals to arise, and in due course for *homo sapiens* to evolve and put the entire world at risk. The next generation or two will have the formidable task of diverting the momentum of human economic behavior into alternative ways for the species to manage its affairs. Truly radical changes are needed, and perhaps an understanding of why behavior can be so difficult to change will help in this endeavor.

End Notes

Chapter 1: Introduction

1. Shahan, T. A., & Burke, K. A. (2004). Ethanol-maintained responding of rats is more resistant to change in a context with added non-drug reinforcement. *Behavioural Pharmacology*, *15*, 279–285.

2. Skinner, B. F. (1938). *The behavior of organisms*. New York: Appleton-Century-Crofts.

3. Pavlov, I. P. (1927). *Conditioned reflexes*. London: Oxford University Press

4. Smith, K. (1974). The continuum of reinforcement and attenuation. *Behaviorism, 2*, 124-145.

Suggested supplementary reading:

Catania, A. C. (2013). *Learning*, (Fifth edition). Cornwall-on-Hudson, NY: Sloan.

Chance, P. (2013) *Learning and Behavior: Active Learning Edition*. Belmont, CA: Wadsworth.

Mazur, J. E. (2005). *Learning and Behavior* (6th Edition). Englewood Cliffs, NJ: Prentice Hall.

Chapter 2: Methods and measures

1. Brown, P. L., & Jenkins, H. M. (1968). Auto-shaping of the pigeon's key-peck. *Journal of the Experimental Analysis of Behavior, 11*, 1-8.

2. Lewis, D. (1952). *Quantitative methods in psychology*. Iowa City, University of Iowa Press.

3. Individual data are also available as Excel spreadsheets from tony.nevin@unh.edu. I urge readers to explore alternative interpretations of these data, and welcome comments and questions.

Suggested supplementary reading:

Daniels, F. (1928). *Mathematical preparation for physical chemistry*. New York: McGraw-Hill. (This was my text in a first-year graduate seminar with Professor Clarence Graham in 1959.)

Shull, R. L. (1991). Mathematical description of operant behavior: an introduction, In I. Iversen & K. A. Lattal (Eds.), *Experimental analysis of behavior* (pp. 243-282). New York: Elsevier. (Especially relevant for this book.)

Madden, J. G., et al., Eds. (2013) *APA Handbook of Behavior Analysis*, Vol. 1; see especially Chapter 7 by Branch and Pennypacker, and Chapter 10 by Dallery and Soto.

Chapter 3: Choice and resistance to change

1. Herrnstein, R. J. (1961). Relative and absolute strength of response as a function of frequency of reinforcement. *Journal of the Experimental Analysis of Behavior, 4*, 267-272. See also Findley, J. D. (1958). Preference and switching under concurrent scheduling. *Journal of the Experimental Analysis of Behavior, 1*, 123-144. Findley arranged concurrent VI VI schedules in a way that made switching between schedules explicit; he did not attempt a quantitative description of his data.

2. Logue, A. W. et al. (2002). The living legacy of the Harvard pigeon lab: Quantitative analysis in the wide world. *Journal of the Experimental Analysis of Behavior, 77*, 357-392.

3. Conger, R., & Killeen, P. (1974). Use of concurrent operants in small group research. *Pacific Sociological Review, 17*, 399-416.

4. Herrnstein, R. J. (1970). On the law of effect. *Journal of the Experimental Analysis of Behavior, 13*, 243- 266.

5. McDowell, J. J (1982). The importance of Herrnstein's mathematical statement of the law of effect for behavior therapy. *American Psychologist, 37*, 771-779.

6. Reynolds, G. S. (1963). Some limitations on contrast and induction during successive discrimination. *Journal of the Experimental Analysis of*

Behavior, 6, 131-139; Shettleworth, S. J. & Nevin, J. A. (1965). Relative rate of response and relative magnitude of reinforcement in multiple schedules. *Journal of the Experimental Analysis of Behavior, 8*, 199-202.

7. Nevin, J. A. (1974). Response strength in multiple schedules. *Journal of the Experimental Analysis of Behavior, 21*, 389-408.

8. Nevin, J. A. (1979). Reinforcement schedules and response strength. In M. D. Zeiler & P. Harzem (Eds.), *Reinforcement and the organization of behaviour* (pp. 117–158). Chichester, England: Wiley.

9. Mace, F. C., Lalli, J. S., Shea, M. C., Lalli, E. P., West, B. J., Roberts, M., & Nevin, J. A. (1990). The momentum of human behavior in a natural setting. *Journal of the Experimental Analysis of Behavior, 54*, 163-172.

10. Cohen, S. L. (1996). Behavioral momentum of typing behavior in college students. *Journal of Behavior Analysis and Therapy, 1*, 36-51.

11. Plaud, J. J. (1996). Human behavioral momentum: Implications for applied behavior analysis and therapy. *Journal of Behavior Therapy and Experimental Psychiatry, 27*, 139-148.

12. Parry-Cruwys, D. E, Neal, C. M., Ahearn, W. H., Wheeler, E. E., Premchander, R., Loeb, M. B., & Dube, W. V. (2011). Resistance to disruption in a classroom setting. *Journal of Applied Behavior Analysis, 44*, 363-367.

Suggested supplementary reading:

Davison, M., & McCarthy, D. (1988). *The matching law: A research review.* Hillsdale, NJ: Erlbaum.

Chapter 4: The momentum metaphor

1. Davison, M., & McCarthy, D. op cit., Ch. 3

2. Nevin, J. A., Mandell, C., & Atak, J. R. (1983). The analysis of behavioral momentum. *Journal of the Experimental Analysis of Behavior, 39*, 49-59.

3. Nevin, J. A., & Grace, R. C. (2000). Behavioral momentum and the Law of Effect. *Behavioral and Brain Sciences, 23*, 73-130.

4. Autor, S. (1960). The strength of conditioned reinforcers as a function of the frequency and probability of reinforcement. In D. P. Hendry (Ed.) *Conditioned reinforcement*. Homewood, IL: Dorsey (pp. 127-162); Grace, R. C. (1994). A contextual model of choice. *Journal of the Experimental Analysis of Behavior, 61*, 113-129.

5. Grace, R. C., Bedell, M. A., & Nevin, J. A. (2002). Preference and resistance to change with constant- and variable-duration terminal links: Independence of reinforcer rate and magnitude. *Journal of the Experimental Analysis of Behavior, 77*, 233-255.

6. Nevin, J. A. (2002). Measuring behavioral momentum. *Behavioural Processes, 57*, 187-198, for discussion of the metric properties of this measure of differential resistance to change.

Chapter 5: Operant and Pavlovian factors

1. Nevin, J. A. (1984). Pavlovian determiners of behavioral momentum. *Animal Learning and Behavior, 12*, 363-370.

2. Williams, B. A. (1979). Contrast, component duration, and the following schedule of reinforcement. *Journal of Experimental Psychology: Animal Behavior Processes, 5*, 379-396; Williams, B. A. (1991). Behavioral contrast and reinforcement value. *Animal Learning and Behavior, 19*, 337-344.

3. Nevin, J. A., Smith, L. D., & Roberts, J. E. (1987). Does contingent reinforcement strengthen operant behavior? *Journal of the Experimental Analysis of Behavior, 48*, 17-33.

4. Gibbon, J. (1981). The contingency problem in autoshaping, In C. M. Locurto, H. S. Terrace, and J. Gibbon (Eds), *Autoshaping and conditioning theory*. New York: Academic Press.

5. Nevin, J. A. (1992). Behavioral contrast and behavioral momentum. *Journal of Experimental Psychology: Animal Behavior Processes, 18*, 126-133.

6. Nevin, J. A., & Grace, R. C. (1999). Does the context of reinforcement affect resistance to change? *Journal of Experimental Psychology: Animal Behavior Processes, 25*, 256-268.

7. Grace, R. C., McLean, A. P., & Nevin, J. A. (2003). Reinforcement context and resistance to change. *Behavioural Processes, 64*, 91–101.

8. Nevin, J. A. (1992). An integrative model for the study of behavioral

momentum. *Journal of the Experimental Analysis of Behavior, 57*, 301–316. See also Nevin, J. A. (2002). op. cit. Ch. 4.

9. Igaki, T., & Sakagami, T. (2004). Resistance to change in goldfish. *Behavioural Processes, 66,* 139-152; Cohen (1996) op. cit. Chapter 3. See also Craig, A. R., Nevin, J. A., & Odum, A. L. (2014). Behavioral momentum and resistance to change. In McSweeney, F. K., & Murphy, E. S. (Eds.),*The Wiley-Blackwell Handbook of Operant and Classical Conditioning.* Oxford, UK: Wiley-Blackwell.

10. Nevin, J. A., Tota, M. E., Torquato, R. D., & Shull, R. L. (1990). Alternative reinforcement increases resistance to change: Pavlovian or operant contingencies? *Journal of the Experimental Analysis of Behavior, 53*, 359-379.

11. Mace et al. (1990) op. cit. Ch. 3.

12. Tota-Faucette, M. E. (1991). *Alternative reinforcement and resistance to change.* Unpublished doctoral dissertation, University of North Carolina, Greensboro.

13. Grimes, J. A., & Shull, R. L. (2001). Response-independent milk delivery enhances persistence of pellet-reinforced lever pressing by rats. *Journal of the Experimental Analysis of Behavior, 76*, 179–194.

14. Mace, F. C., McComas, J. J., Mauro, B. C., Progar, P. R., Ervin, R., & Zangrillo, A. N. (2010). Differential reinforcement of alternative behavior increases resistance to extinction: Clinical demonstration, animal modeling, and clinical test of one solution. *Journal of the Experimental Analysis of Behavior, 93*, 349-367.

Chapter 6: Challenges

1. Craig, A. R., Nevin, J. A., & Odum, A. L. (2014) op. cit. Ch. 5.

2. Blackman, D. E. (1968). Response rate, reinforcement frequency, and conditioned suppression. *Journal of the Experimental Analysis of Behavior, 11*, 503-516.

3. Nevin (1974) op. cit. Ch. 3.

4. Lattal, K. A. (1989). Contingencies on response rate and resistance to change. *Learning and Motivation, 20*, 191-203.

5. Fath, S. J., Fields, L., Malott, M. K., & Grossett, D. (1983). Response

rate, latency, and resistance to change. *Journal of the Experimental Analysis of Behavior, 39,* 267–274.

6. Nevin, J. A., Grace, R. C., Holland, S., & McLean, A. P. (2001). Variable-ratio versus variable-interval schedules: Response rate, resistance to change and preference. *Journal of the Experimental Analysis of Behavior, 76,* 43-74.

7. Bell, M. C. (1999). Pavlovian contingencies and resistance to change in a multiple schedule. *Journal of the Experimental Analysis of Behavior, 72,* 81-96; Bell had presented these data at the 1996 meetings of the Association or Behavior Analysis. Grace, R. C., Schwendiman, J. W., & Nevin, J. A. (1998). Effects of unsignaled delay of reinforcement on preference and resistance to change. *Journal of the Experimental Analysis of Behavior, 69,* 247-261.

8. Fantino, E. (1969). Effects of required rates of responding upon choice. *Journal of the Experimental Analysis of Behavior, 11,* 15-22.

9. Nevin (1979) op. cit. Ch. 3.

10. Mandell, C. (1980). Response strength in multiple periodic and aperiodic schedules. *Journal of the Experimental Analysis of Behavior, 33,* 221-241; Mellon, R. C., & Shull, R. D. (1986). Resistance to change produced by access to fixed-delay versus variable-delay terminal links. *Journal of the Experimental Analysis of Behavior, 46,* 79-92.

11. Podlesnik, C. A., Jimenez-Gomez, C., Thrailkill, E. A., & Shahan, T. A. (2011). Temporal context, preference, and resistance to change. *Journal of the Experimental Analysis of Behavior, 96.* 191-213.

12. McLean, A. P., Grace, R. C., & Nevin, J. A. (2012). Response strength in extreme multiple schedules. *Journal of the Experimental Analysis of Behavior, 97,* 51-70.

13. Cohen, S. L., Riley, D. S. & Weigle, P. A. (1993) Tests of behavior momentum in simple and multiple schedules with rats and pigeons. *Journal of the Experimental Analysis of Behavior, 60,* 255-291.

14. Cohen, S. L. (1998) Behavioral momentum: The effects of temporal separation of rates of reinforcement. *Journal of the Experimental Analysis of Behavior, 69,* 29-47.

15. Lionello-DeNolf, K. M., & Dube, W. V. (2011). Contextual influences on resistance to disruption in children with intellectual disabilities. *Journal of the Experimental Analysis of Behavior, 96,* 317-327.

Chapter 7: Extinction

1. vom Saal, W. (1972). Choice between stimuli previously presented separately. *Learning and Motivation, 3*, 200-222.

2. Nevin, J. A., & Grace, R. C. (2005). Resistance to extinction in the steady state and in transition. *Journal of Experimental Psychology: Animal Behavior Processes, 31*, 199-212.

3. Nevin, J. A. (1988) Behavioral momentum and the partial reinforcement effect. *Psychological Bulletin, 103*, 44-56.

4. Gallistel, C. R., & Gibbon, J. (2000). Time, rate, and conditioning. *Psychological Review, 107*, 289-344.

5. Shull, R. L., & Grimes, J. A. (2006). Resistance to extinction following variable-interval reinforcement: Reinforcer rate and amount. *Journal of the Experimental Analysis of Behavior, 85*, 23-39.

6. Catania, A. C. (1973). The nature of learning. In J. A. Nevin & G. S. Reynolds (Eds.) *The study of behavior: Learning, Motivation, Emotion, and Instinct.* Glenview, IL: Scott Foresman (pp. 31-68). See especially pp. 48-50.

7. Nevin & Grace (2000) op. cit. Ch. 4.

8. Nevin, J. A., McLean, A. P., & Grace, R. C. (2001). Resistance to extinction: Contingency termination and generalization decrement. *Animal Learning and Behavior, 29*, 176-191.

9. Grace, R. C., McLean, A. P., & Nevin, J. A. (2003) op. cit. Ch. 5.

10. Koegel, R. L., & Rincover, A. (1977). Research on the difference between generalization and maintenance in extra-therapy responding. *Journal of Applied Behavior Analysis, 10*, 1-12.

11. MacDonald, J. M., Ahearn, W. H., Parry-Cruwys, D., Bancroft, S., & Dube, W. V. (2013). Persistence during extinction: Examining the effects of continuous and intermittent reinforcement on problem behavior. *Journal of Applied Behavior Analysis, 46*, 333-338.

12. Nevin (1974) op. cit. Ch. 3

13. Thanks to Amy Odum and students in the Psych 3400 lab course at USU.

14. Podlesnik, C. R., & Shahan, T. A. (2009). Behavioral momentum and re-lapse of extinguished operant responding. *Learning and Behavior, 37,* 357-364.

15. Shahan, T. A., & Sweeney, M. M. (2011). A model of resurgence based on behavioral momentum theory. *Journal of the Experimental Analysis of Behavior, 95,* 91–108.

16. Volkert, V. M., Lerman, D. C., Call., N. A., & Trosclair-Lasserre, N. (2009). An evaluation of resurgence during treatment with functional communication training. *Journal of Applied Behavior Analysis, 42,* 145-160.

17. Wacker, D. P., Harding, J. W., Berg, W. K., Lee, J. F., Schieltz, K. M., Padilla, Y. C., Nevin, J. A., & Shahan, T. A. (2011). *Journal of the Experimental Analysis of Behavior, 96,* 261-282.

Chapter 8: Conditional discrimination

1. Cumming, W. W, & Berryman, R. (1965). The complex discriminated operant: Studies of matching-to-sample and related problems. In D. Mostovsk (Ed.) *Stimulus Generalization.* Stanford University Press, Stanford, CA (pp. 284-330).

2. Davison, M. C., & Tustin, R. D. (1978). The relation between the gen-eralized matching law and signal-detection theory. *Journal of the Experimental Analysis of Behavior, 29,* 331-336.

3. Davison, M., & Nevin, J. A. (1999). Stimuli, reinforcers, and behavior: An integration. *Journal of the Experimental Analysis of Behavior, 71,* 439-482.

4. Schaal, D. W., Odum, A. L., & Shahan, T. A. (2000). Pigeons may not remember the stimuli that reinforced their behavior. *Journal of the Experimental Analysis of Behavior, 73,* 125-139.

5. Nevin, J. A., Milo, J., Odum, A. L., & Shahan, T. A. (2003). Accuracy of discrimination, rate of responding, and resistance to change. *Journal of the Experimental Analysis of Behavior, 79,* 307-321.

6. Odum, A. L., Shahan, T. A., & Nevin, J. A. (2005). Resistance to change of forgetting functions and response rates. *Journal of the Experimental Analysis of Behavior, 84,* 65-75.

7. Peterson, G. B., Wheeler, R. L., & Trapold, M. A. (1980). Expectan-cies as mediators in the differential-reward conditional discrimination performance of pigeons. *Animal Learning and Behavior, 8,* 22-30.

8. Nevin, J. A., Ward, R. D., Jimenez-Gomez, C., Odum, A. L., & Shahan, T. A. (2009). Differential outcomes enhance accuracy of delayed matching to sample but not resistance to change. *Journal of Experimental Psychology: Animal Behavior Processes, 35*, 74-91.

9. Litt, M. D., & Schreibman, L. (1981). Stimulus-specific reinforcement in the acquisition of receptive labels by autistic children. *Analysis and Intervention in Developmental Disabilities, 1*, 171-186.

10. www.theinvisiblegorilla.com/gorilla_experiment.html

11. Dube, W. V., & McIlvane, W. J. (1997). Reinforcer frequency and restricted stimulus control. *Journal of the Experimental Analysis of Behavior, 68*, 303-316.

12. Shahan, T. A., & Podlesnik, C. A. (2006). Divided attention performance and the matching law. *Learning and Behavior, 34*, 255-261.

13. Podlesnik, C. A., Thrailkill, E, & Shahan, T. A. (2012). Differential reinforcement and resistance to change of divided-attention performance. *Learning and Behavior, 40*, 158–169.

14. Nevin, J. A., Davison, M., Odum, A. L., & Shahan, T. A. (2007). A theory of attending, remembering, and reinforcement in delayed matching to sample. *Journal of the Experimental Analysis of Behavior, 88*, 285-317.

15. Brown, G. S., & White, K. G. (2009). Reinforcer probability, reinforcer magnitude, and the reinforcement context for remembering. *Journal of Experimental Psychology: Animal Behavior Processes, 35*, 238–249.

16. Nevin, J. A., Shahan, T. A., Odum, A. L., & Ward, R. (2012). Delayed matching to sample: Reinforcement has opposite effects on resistance to change in two related procedures. *Learning and Behavior, 40*, 380-392.

17. Skinner, B. F. (1969). *Contingencies of reinforcement: A theoretical analysis.* New York: Appleton-Century-Crofts. Reprinted by B. F. Skinner Foundation, Acton, MA: XanEdu Publishing Inc. (2013).

Chapter 9: Extensions

1. Mace, F. C., Hock, M. L., Lalli, J. S., West, P. J.,Belfiore, P., Pinter, E., & Brown, D. K. (1988). Behavioral momentum in the treatment of non-compliance. *Journal of Applied Behavior Analysis, 21*, 123-141.

2. Lee, D. L., Belfiore, P. J., Scheeler, M. C., Hua, Y., & Smith, R. (2004). Behavioral momentum in academics: Using embedded high-p sequences to increase academic productivity. *Psychology in the Schools, 41*, 789-801. For other examples see Davis, C. A., Brady, M. P., Hamilton, R., McEvoy, M A., & Williams, R. E. (1994). Effects of high-probability requests on the social interactions of young children with severe disabilities. *Journal of Applied Behavior Analysis, 27*, 619-637; DuCharme J. M., & Worling, D. E. (1994). Behavioral momentum and stimulus fading in the acquisition and maintenance of child compliance in the home. *Journal of Applied Behavior Analysis, 27*, 639-647;

3. Mace et al. (2010) op. cit. Ch. 5

4. Podlesnik, C. A., Bai, J. H. Y., & Elliffe, D. (2012). Resistance to extinction and relapse in combined stimulus contexts. *Journal of the Experimental Analysis of Behavior, 98*, 169-189.

5. Donlin, W. D., Knealing, T. W., Needham, M., Wong , C. J. & Silverman, K. (2008). Attendance Rates in a Workplace Predict Subsequent Outcome of Employment-Based Reinforcement of Cocaine Abstinence in Methadone Patients. *Journal of Applied Behavior Analysis, 41*, 499-516; Higgins, S. T., Wong, C. J., Badger, G. J., Ogden, D. E. H. , & Dantona, R. L. (2000). Contingent Reinforcement Increases Cocaine Abstinence During Outpatient Treatment and 1 Year of Follow-Up. *Journal of Consulting and Clinical Psychology, 68*, 64-72;

Postscript

1. Holman, S. W. (1898). *Matter, energy, force, and work.* New York: Mac-Millan.

2. Neuringer, A. & Jensen, G. (2010). Operant variability and voluntary action. *Psychological Review, 117*, 972-993; Rakos, R. F., Laurence, K. R., Skala, S., & Slane, S. (2008). Belief in free will: Measurement and conceptualization innovations. *Behavior and Social Issues. 17*, 20-39.

3. Nevin, J. A. (1989). Recent advances in the experimental analysis of behavior. In A. Brownstein (Ed.), *Progress in behavioral studies.* Hillsdale, NJ: Erlbaum.

4. Some of this material is adapted from a talk at the 2004 meetings of the Association for Behavior Analysis, later published as Nevin, J. A. (2005). The inertia of affluence. *Behavior and Social Issues, 14*, 7-20. The

title phrase comes from Bill McKibben's article, "The end of nature," which appeared in *The New Yorker*, Sept. 11, 1989.

5. Skinner, B. F. (1981). Selection by consequences. *Science, 213*, 501-504.

6. Kolbert, E. (2014). *The sixth extinction*. New York: Henry Holt.

www.ingramcontent.com/pod-product-compliance
Lightning Source LLC
Chambersburg PA
CBHW070856290526
45795CB00001B/146